Father Figure

My Mission to Prevent Child Sexual Abuse

Marfa House
Marfa, Texas

Marfa House
Marfa, Texas

Father Figure
My Mission to Prevent Child Sexual Abuse

Published by Marfa House

All Rights Reserved

Copyright 2014, 2017 by Sumi Mukherjee
(2nd Edition)

ISBN: 978-1-946072-30-6

ALSO BY SUMI MUKHERJEE:

A Life Interrupted – The Story of my Battle With Bullying and Obsessive Compulsive Disorder

How to Stand Up to Workplace Bullying and Take on an Unjust Employer

Table of Contents

Reviews

I have been working on the prevention and mitigation of child sexual abuse (CSA) for 14 years. The level of CSA occurring throughout our nation and the world is staggering and often devastating. And most of it occurs by people who know and have access to the child on a regular basis, including an extraordinary number of family members - a good part of the difficulty in addressing it. Unfortunately, the closer we get to "home," literally and figuratively, the less likely we are to deal with it due to the personal shame, the unavoidable involvement of family and/or community members, and the responsibility of caretakers of the child. Child sexual abuse, unlike breast cancer, which had its own battle to emerge into the light of discussion and research and societal address, is someone's and often more than one person's fault.

Something needs to change – in fact, a lot needs to change and we have to be able to get individuals and our societal systems to "listen" and act.

Father Figure by Sumi Mukherjee is a brilliant and captivating piece of storytelling – through the medium of a very important and poignant personal tale, but it is much more. In a manner that draws us in to "witness," sympathize, and empathize with the personal lives of Mr. Mukherjee and the adults and children who Mr. Mukherjee came to know, Father Figure provides key information, salient advice, and guidance on what child sexual abuse is, what it does, how it happens, how to recognize it, what to do about it, and how to prevent it. The story more than holds one's interest, as it needs to do in order to get people to "listen" and wake up to what is happening all around us, and act! Now, with information available through mediums like Mukherjee's Father Figure, perhaps we will!

Pamela Pine, PhD, MPH
Founder and CEO
Stop the Silence: Stop Child Sexual Abuse
Glenn Dale, MD

Father Figure gives a riveting account of how a family friend chose not to give up until justice was served for two defenseless little girls, who were possibly in line to be preyed upon by their mother's boyfriend...a "registered sex offender". This man hid in plain sight... in the home with his potential victims... while on probation for being convicted of a molestation crime he committed against an 11-year old girl.

Studies have shown that sexual violence is a vicious cycle. This book goes into great detail highlighting the behavior of an adult who is likely a survivor of childhood molestation. This vicious cycle seems to continue particularly for the survivors who did not get the counseling they desperately needed as children.

If a victim is "not believed" as a child, if they "weren't given the opportunity to disclose" their victimization in a safe environment, or if they did not get the counseling they needed as a child to work through the trauma of being victimized by their predator, the cycle seems to continue. This book gives a snapshot of the life of a mom who seems to repeat a pattern that could be harmful for herself and her children.

This book is captivating. It gives an account of how a family friend believed in the cause of keeping those girls safe and worked tirelessly with family, friends, law enforcement, the justice court system, and other interested organizations such as child protection system and rape and sexual abuse crisis center. It's educational and loaded with resources that will educate the reader on the dos and don'ts of single moms dating in the 21st century. Most importantly it tells the true story of a "father figure" who worked tirelessly to save two girls from a possible scenario of abuse by a convicted sexual predator. The book also makes a key point that 'prevention' means doing something before it happens – it means avoiding a scenario that might lead to possible abuse.

Bevelyn Mitchell
Rape Crisis Center
Myrtle Beach, SC

The account of this mission was riveting. The ways that he relived so many of these harrowing experiences on his mission to protect children must have been exhausting, yet he persevered to bring attention to a very personal matter.

Although the purpose of this book is to educate the public and prevent sexual abuse of children, I felt that is was written in such a way that it was healing to the author in a very personal fashion. What a triumphant message this book is sending the reader, the abuser and the victims. The author took on a huge risk becoming so involved with this family, but his dedication and desire to help proved to be triumphant for many and a wake-up call to some.

Ellen Olsson
Safe Homes, Inc.
Winfield, KS

Acknowledgments

First and foremost - on a personal level - I would like to thank my family and friends whose presence over the years has helped me reach my potential and to now try and help others.

My very special thanks go to Ashley McCormick, an experienced social worker who reviewed my manuscript and provided helpful insight and excellent comments, feedback and advice. I was delighted to have this helpful perspective and to incorporate suggestions into the book. I would also like to thank Dr. Pamela Pine, PhD, MPH, Founder and CEO, Stop the Silence: Stop Child Sexual Abuse, Glenn Dale, MD, for her review of the manuscript and for a number of excellent comments that I decided to incorporate within the manuscript.

My very special thanks go to Bevelyn Mitchell, Rape Crisis Center, Myrtle Beach, SC, for her support in reviewing the manuscript and for her help in organizing speaking opportunities on this topic.

My very special thanks also go to Ellen Olsson, Safe Homes Inc, Winfield, KS, for her review of the manuscript and for her willingness to organize speaking opportunities.

I would also like to thank Sonia Miller-Van Oort, Attorney & Founder at Sapientia Law Group in Minneapolis, MN, for her legal support of this book.

Dedication

This book is dedicated to all people around the world who are working hard to prevent child sexual abuse.

Father Figure: My Mission to Prevent Child Sexual Abuse

"Anyone can give up, it's the easiest thing in the world to do. But to hold it together when everyone else would understand if you fell apart, that's true strength."

-Viktor Frankl

Preface

The following account is based on a true story. Besides using my own real name, I have created pseudonyms (fictitious names) for all of the other characters involved to protect their identities. I have also chosen not to name the cities and/or state in which these real-life events took place for the very same reason.

The purpose of this book is to educate the public and prevent sexual abuse of children. While the entire account is captivating, the final chapter serves to reinforce what the public should learn from this story: including essential advice for ordinary citizens, caregivers of children and kids who are being victimized. Please check out the "helpful resources" list at the back of the book as well.

This book is for Lisa and Laura, the two main kids featured in this story, whom I love dearly and whom it seems I have now lost. I miss you a lot and think fondly about all of our good times. I hope you are safe, doing well and happy in your lives. I hope that one day in the future I may be able to see you both again.

This book is for Mark, Mike, Tim, and all the special children in my life whom I love as if they were my own.

This book is also for every child out there who is currently suffering from sexual abuse. To all of you who are, PLEASE find the courage, which you do have buried deep down inside of you, to tell someone you trust; an adult at your school, a sexual assault crisis phone hotline worker, a true friend, someone who you know will have your back. For more helpful information, please be sure to review the first subsection of Chapter 23, titled "Silent Victims." This book was written for you.

Chapter One

My Life as a Father Figure

Being raised by the two best parents I could have possibly asked for, family times growing up were by far the happiest times of my life. Blessed as I was at home, this is also a sad statement, as my teen years and adulthood would soon be plagued with hardship and pain. The child of immigrant parents from India, I was raised in the Midwestern part of the United States in the 1980s and 1990s. Though I was born in Canada in May of 1976, I've lived in the U.S. for my entire life, since about nine months of age.

Though my home life was overall wonderful, I had an extremely difficult time throughout school. From kindergarten onward, I quickly became aware of the fact that I was viewed as being different from nearly all of my peers due to my race and ethnicity. As I got older, I was bullied on a regular basis for being brown skinned, for being the child of Indian immigrants, and for having such a markedly unusual name. Over time, many years of bullying led to Post Traumatic Stress Disorder (PTSD) and set the stage for the development of severe Obsessive-Compulsive Disorder (OCD) at the tender age of sixteen.

Ages sixteen to twenty-one were by far the worst years of my life, as I struggled silently with my OCD symptoms, afraid that I was losing my mind. At twenty-one, I finally broke my long-held silence and began receiving OCD treatment, a process that would take many more years from my life. At twenty-four, I took a major step toward recovery in deciding to look up and confront the one individual who had bullied me the most intensely during my childhood. Incredibly, it was the mental image of this bully's face that my OCD would most frequently use to torment me. With the confrontation a tremendous success, I continued in my OCD recovery and was fortunate enough to publish my autobiography in July 2011 documenting my inspiring story titled, "A Life Interrupted: The Story Of My Battle With Bullying And Obsessive-Compulsive Disorder."

While the title for the book is certainly catchy, a life interrupted is exactly what I'd received. Unlike most young adults in America, I lived with my parents and remained isolated until the age of twenty-seven. These were the additional years that I spent struggling with my mental illness and slowly learning to overcome it. Along with working numerous hotel jobs, I also took college courses during this time in subjects such as psychology, sociology, criminal justice, corrections (prison system), and childcare.

I also began dating around the age of twenty-seven, which was in 2003, and quickly discovered that my race and ethnicity would once again work strongly against me. Soon I found myself meeting many rejections by potential partners, some of whom made it clear that my race was indeed the issue. Most tragic of all, even those who appeared to take interest in me would eventually just back away. There was one in particular who had truly broken my heart. This was the person with whom I had longed to get married and start a new life, but it seemed as though my dreams of having a family were just not to be.

Somewhere along the way I left the hotel business and entered the field of childcare, in May 2007. This abrupt change in career choice stemmed from a lengthy dating relationship I had with a single mother of a nine-year-old boy, beginning in 2004 and lasting until 2011. In the course of our interactions, I came to learn that her young son had been physically abused and abandoned by his father, my girlfriend's ex-husband. I would later find out that an older male cousin had also sexually abused him repeatedly. Neither the father, who would later commit suicide, nor the older male cousin, was ever held accountable for their maltreatment of this little boy.

When I first met this woman and her son in late 2004, the angry child was exhibiting extremely challenging behavior on a very regular basis. In fact, my girlfriend was at her wit's end and honestly did not know what to do, but we soon found that my involvement in this young man's life, as a positive father figure, brought out some truly spectacular changes. Over a period of time, everyone who encountered us would comment on how much better this child was now doing, and how the difference in his behavior was like between night and day. Seeing what a positive impact I was having, I began unofficially mentoring several other young friends of this boy who were also dealing with problems. Before very long, I became a father figure to them as well.

Enjoying my ability to make such an amazing difference, I decided to try to turn my new passion into a full-time career. After volunteering with two community organizations that catered to troubled youth, I was awarded the "Volunteer Of The Year" award by one of them and subsequently hired in May 2007. At my job, some of the kids would say they wished that I was their father. One eager youngster even told me to try and ask out his mom! As a person who was blessed with having the most incredible Dad, it was easy for me to give back to those kids who had not been as lucky in life.

Unfortunately, things would eventually begin to sour between my girlfriend and me. In fact, one of the biggest issues we faced as a couple was when my girlfriend wanted to allow her son to be around his older male cousin again, the same one who I understood had repeatedly raped and molested him in the past. Naturally, I strenuously objected to this proposition, and quickly found myself at war with my girlfriend's immediate and extended family members. They all rallied unconditionally behind the older male cousin, as he was also a part of their family. Worst of all was the fact that my girlfriend's young son also started siding with his alleged former molester. By April 2011, the friction was too much to handle, and my relationship with this woman eventually came to an end. Although there were other issues which also led to our separation, this one certainly played a key role in making things harder for us.

Remarkably, our breakup did not mark the conclusion to that story. I would later learn, from viewing our state's prison website, that this same older male cousin had gone on to commit a brand new sexual crime, and this time around he wasn't able to get away with it. As of July 2012, the older male cousin was incarcerated with a three-year sentence at a medium-security state prison, this time for molesting a young girl between the ages of thirteen and fifteen. The expiration date on his potential full sentence and probationary period is incredibly set for the month of June in the year 2116! My gut instinct about the older male cousin had, of course, been correct all along.

After leaving the childcare field and then getting my first book published, I focused my efforts on establishing myself as an author and a public speaker. Following my breakup in April 2011, I also began using a popular online dating service in an effort to meet single women. In doing so, I soon made a connection with a lady who lived in a very small town in my state that I didn't even know existed. This little town was more than fifty miles away from the one in which I reside, and was about a one-hour drive by car.

I didn't know much about this new dating prospect, other than that the picture she posted of herself on the dating website looked reasonably attractive. I also came to learn that her name was Kim, and that she was interested in meeting sometime soon. So on Friday, May 6, 2011, which happened to be my 35th birthday, I communicated with Kim by email, and then we decided to meet up that night.

Little did I realize at that time that I'd be meeting a most unique woman.

Chapter Two

Meeting a Most Unique Woman

The near-hour-long drive to Kim's small town was a bit confusing for me, as it was nighttime and I had never traveled this route before, but after a little trouble due to poor signage, I was finally able to locate Kim's house in her far-away neighborhood.

Upon greeting Kim for the first time at her front door, I immediately noticed that she looked somewhat different from the picture she had posted on the dating website. Regardless, Kim came across as quite friendly and interested. From her home, Kim and I then went to a nearby restaurant and sat down to have dinner together.

As we began to get better acquainted, Kim told me that she had a rare genetic condition that had rendered her legally blind, and that she was unable to operate a motor vehicle. Therefore, she relied fully on her parents, who lived close by, and friends for her transportation.

While I told Kim about myself and the end of my previous relationship, she, in turn, filled me in on what her life was all about. She told me that she was a divorced, single mother with two young daughters Lisa, age eleven, and Laura, age eight. She explained that her marriage with the girls' father, Dave, had ended supposedly due to his frequent drug use, his collection of drug paraphernalia, and his unhealthy obsession with viewing pornography. Kim said he was not a good dad to their daughters, and that the daughters did not like him that much. She explained that her daughters were currently with their father that weekend, as Dave was granted parenting time every other weekend and four hours on Wednesday evenings. Kim also said she had ended a three-year relationship in December with a different man who had lived with her and her daughters through much of that time.

After dinner, Kim and I returned to her house to relax and have a few beers. Though I wasn't a regular drinker partially due to my OCD medications, but it was my birthday after all, and she was quick to make the offer. Along with giving me a tour of her home, Kim then told me all about her young daughters. I immediately observed their pictures hanging on the wall by the dining table, and noted that both girls were quite pretty with a special brightness about them. Over the course of the evening, she showed me several photos of her children taken through the years, from when they were just little ones up until now. She told me how Laura had broken her arm once in the past, and showed me a photo from when that occurred. She also showed me one picture of her daughters taking a bath together when they were much younger. These actions by Kim, in allowing me to learn more about her daughters and see these pictures, will pick up greater significance later on in this book.

As the evening progressed, Kim went on her computer and showed me the description of her rare genetic condition on Wikipedia. Along with confirming that I wasn't going to hold her condition against her, I also let her know that I wasn't at all opposed to dating a single mother. My recent ex-girlfriend, of course, was a single mother and I had no trouble accepting her son in my life. Over a short period of time things began escalating between Kim and me.

With things off to a fantastic start between us, she offered me the opportunity to meet her daughters in the very near future. Naturally, I accepted the invitation and we planned to get together the next week. Although I was very used to being around kids at this point in my life, getting to know Kim's girls would prove to be one heck of a ride.

Chapter Three

Two Gifts That I Wasn't Expecting

Meeting Lisa and Laura was an interesting experience, to put it rather mildly. Yet, it was one that would forever change my life and fill it with warmth, joy, thrill, and happiness that I had not known in some time. That's because I did not merely meet two new people on Tuesday, May 10, 2011, but rather I had been blessed with two special gifts that I wasn't expecting.

Lisa and Laura were two remarkably intense, lively, young forces to be reckoned with. They were outrageous; spunky; wild; energetic; adventurous; fearless; funny; and violent, mostly toward each other and eventually toward me as well, but after they got to know me. On the very first day I met them, I witnessed numerous fights; struggles; chases; and aggressive verbal exchanges between the two sisters.

What struck and impressed me by far about these mostly playful encounters was the fact that cute little Laura simply refused to back down from a fight. While many younger siblings had the sense to back off when the older one got assertive, Laura could not and would not, stand for having her basic rights infringed upon in any manner. At one point during a spat, I even confronted her about it and asked her, "Laura, why do you always choose to hit or kick Lisa back, when you know she's bigger than you and is going to eventually squash you?"

Without a second's doubt or hesitation, Laura turned to me full of self-assurance and replied, "Because I've decided that, **'that's what she gets!'**" I figured she had a good point.

While older sister Lisa left the house for some time that day, I had more of a chance to get to know Laura better on our first meeting, and what I got to know better than anything else was how remarkably silly she could be. As I sat on the couch next to mother and daughter, little Laura kept grabbing her mother's face playfully and saying, "WHAT'S YOUR NAME?!" in a really funny voice, drawing out the letters. When she wasn't doing that, she would repeatedly thrust her fingers in the air and exclaim, "ROCK'N'ROLL EVERYBODY!" over and over again. At one point Kim asked if Laura was acting this way due to feeling awkward around me, a total stranger in her house, and I was surprised when Laura cheerfully smiled and replied, "Oh, no worries, man."

There were indeed worries in the mind of poor Kim. Concerned that her daughter's goofy behavior may scare me away, she kept trying to ask Laura why she was apparently in such "rare form" on this particular afternoon. It sure didn't help Kim any when Laura shot back, "but I'm always this way!"

Aside from their silly antics and playful aggression, the biggest thing that struck me about Lisa and Laura was how they both appeared starved for the love and attention of a father figure. As I continued to date Kim and spend more time with her daughters, the girls and I quickly developed a very fun and close relationship. I'd always loved kids and been excellent with them, and they had always seemed to love me just as much in return. I was surprised how little time it took before they were both warming up to me and hopping on my back for piggyback rides. When I took Kim and her girls to a water park hotel at the end of May 2011, Lisa asked if I would let her ride on my back as I swam around the pool in a circle, several times. She felt a bit heavy at certain moments, and it turned out to be a good little workout for me. Even though she was about to turn twelve, Lisa seemed to enjoy having me fulfill that father role, as of course did I. "Boy, you two have really connected well this weekend," Kim remarked, in reference to Lisa and I. "She didn't connect like this with her father, or my ex-boyfriend who lived with us for three years!"

Kim voiced similar appreciation one evening when Lisa invited me into her bedroom to take a look at all the posters she had taped up on her walls. "She never let any of the other guys enter her room, which is her private domain," Kim commented.

Though Lisa seemed to have a difficult time in expressing or exchanging deep emotion, she would often show her affection for me through insults and name-calling. "Oh, Sumi, you're a dumbass and a pussy!" she would often say as she sat next to me and/or solicited a piggyback ride. I felt that this was her obnoxious, pre-teen manner of showing that she was starting to care.

Laura and I also had a very special connection, and it was rooted in the use of humor to entertain. She was an extremely goofy child blessed with having a tremendous sense of humor, and she always seemed to have an expression on her face as though she was about to burst into giggles. In fact, making Laura crack up uncontrollably became one of our favorite hobbies. Whether she would be hitting me, kicking me or pulling the hairs on my chest, back, arms, and legs, I would make a funny face like I was in agony and she would fall to the floor in laughter. It was so easy to make her laugh through my facial expressions, and in turn, her laughter was so infectious that I couldn't resist but to lose it myself.

There were so many moments when Kim was trying to make a serious point to Laura or enforce discipline, but she would always succeed at getting her mom to break down by mimicking Kim and making her lose her composure. "You might try to help me a little here!" Kim would say to me, half frustrated, but in my defense, I was laughing too hard to be of any assistance.

What made these silly incidents most enjoyable was the fact that they served as an indication of a growing relationship. On Father's Day in June 2011, Kim texted me to specially share that little Laura had asked her whether or not I was a father. When Kim replied that I wasn't, she said Laura looked up at her and responded by saying thoughtfully, "Well, he really should be." That's a text that I have saved on my old phone still to this day.

However, by early July 2011 things between Kim and me had begun to sour. As much as I loved her daughters and vice versa, I found my dating relationship with Kim to be less than ideal. Eventually, she broke up with me without explanation on the Fourth of July, and I lost contact with her and the girls for several months. Then in mid-November 2011, I heard from Kim again out of the blue, and she now said that she wanted to resume a friendship with me.

In early December 2011, after five months of no contact, I was reunited with Kim and her girls at the celebration party for Laura's 9th birthday. In spite of the time lapse since having seen each other, I was moved by how quickly both girls embraced me back into their lives, no questions asked. Though Kim would go on to pressure me to resume our dating relationship, I had wised up a bit following our sudden breakup. I repeatedly told her that I loved her and her girls dearly, but that it would be better if she and I stayed good friends. In due course, it certainly seemed as though she and I did better with friendship.

With things going well, I began visiting Kim and her girls again on a regular basis. Once again there were enjoyable outings, road trips and stays at hotels, as well as all of our usual great times and camaraderie, along with the normal ups and downs of a child/parent relationship with my role as the father figure.

Before long, two special neighborhood boys would join our hilarious group.

Chapter Four

Neighbor Boys Join in the Action

Best friends often say that it feels as though they have known each other forever, but in the case of sisters Lisa and Laura and the two brothers who lived across the street from them, it was literally the truth. From the time they were all in diapers, these four kids would play together almost every day, on the same street in the small town they all grew up in.

Kim's neighbors across the street, the parents of these two boys, were a couple named James and Joan. Their long relationship as neighbors began back when Kim was married to Dave, the father of her girls and while he was still living with them. James and Joan actually had three sons, one older boy and then the two younger ones, who were both close in age to one another, as well as to Lisa and Laura.

I first had the pleasure of meeting the boys when I had been dating Kim, between May and July 2011. Our contact began with the then shy, quiet Mark wandering around Kim's house on certain occasions when I was visiting or about to take Kim and her girls out somewhere. I found Mark to be an extremely intelligent, sensitive, kind-hearted young man, with whom I soon developed a positive connection. At some point, Kim's girls and I began inviting Mark to come along with us on fun outings. I soon met the boys' parents, and they had no problem with Mark accompanying us. Before long I also met the athletic, younger brother, Mike, and he began to join us as well.

`Though Kim's girls and these boys would often flirt with one another, they truly regarded each other as siblings in every sense. Oh sure, they would fight like cats and dogs and complain about each other at length, yet they couldn't resist playing together on an almost daily basis. Not an occasion would go by (unless they happened to be feuding) when the girls wouldn't ask if the boys could also join us during our outings.

The boys would accompany us on a regular basis, and much more so after we were all reunited in December 2011. We were all going to movies, water parks, hotels, arcades, zoos, bowling, swimming, amusement parks, and any other fun activity one can think of. For my 36th birthday, in May 2012, I rented a limo and surprised the four kids by bringing it into their neighborhood.

Kim had been in on this elaborate plan as well, and together we had tricked her girls into believing that singer Demi Lovato was passing through their tiny town. Because Kim's job at times allowed for her to come into contact with celebrities, she and I were able to make our story quite convincing. As Kim and her girls waited with cameras on their front lawn, the girls were perhaps a little disappointed to find out that the "celebrity" arriving was just me. "Oh, Mom, I can't believe you tricked us like that!" They both exclaimed with dismay. Lisa, who typically chided others for being gullible, had been beaten this time around.

The boys' presence only served to increase the level of excitement and hilariousness among the children. A group mentality quickly took over, and I must admit that at times I was a key player in egging on rowdy, outrageous behavior. I had also grown to relish my role as the provider of this entertainment, and developed a weakness when it came to keeping things under control. However, I also knew that it was up to me, as the father figure, to maintain an overall sense of responsibility.

There were soon occasions where Kim wanted a break from her girls and did not accompany us, and it was just the foursome and I. On such days, the kids and I came up with a saying, "What happens in Sumi's car, **'stays'** in Sumi's car," which we quoted freely among each other to summarize our naughty camaraderie. It was the playful code we used to remind one another to keep our silliness on the down low. Though I cherished our carefree moments, I was also mindful about making sure that our fun activities remained within acceptable responsible boundaries. At some point, Kim began to ask me to help with watching her girls on a more regular basis, especially when she had to work on weekends that her girls were staying with her. Naturally, I accepted the offer as my schedule permitted, and the girls and I would then round up the boys and we'd all have a fabulous time. "I never had so much fun in my life until I met you, Sumi!" was a comment made to me by Mike that really touched my heart.

It's, of course, important to note that in spite of some rowdy endeavors, our whole relationship was based upon mutual love and affection. There was a time when Mark told me that I was the nicest guy he had ever met in his life. Humbled and touched, I asked him what made him draw that conclusion. "Well, you do all this great stuff for us, you take care of us, and you handle things so fairly each time when there's fighting among us. I think of you Sumi, as being my second dad, right next to my actual father." It wasn't long before his brother Mike would make similar statements.

When I was tucking the children into bed one night at my house, Mike actually said "Goodnight Dad," to me, which really surprised me. I was further moved when the remaining three children then also said the same thing. Soon, both Lisa and Laura would refer to me as being their "Dad" on a regular basis. On one occasion, little Laura even told me she saw me as being her "Super Hero."

As great as all the good times with the kids truly were, there were also certain things about the girls and their lives that really concerned me. As close as I had become to this family, I couldn't help observing the bad right along with the good; the disturbing right along with the normal. While I tried to look past such worries whenever they arose, over time it seemed to get harder to ignore the concerns.

15

Chapter Five

Concerns Looming Under the Surface

I'm sure most of us have heard the widespread belief that all jokes contain hidden truth. In fact, according to an essay titled "Humor," published by the head of the Anthropology Department at Brown University, Dr. William Beeman says that Sigmund Freud proposed there are only two reasons for jokes; 1) hostility, insult, verbal assault; and 2) to expose the person who is the subject of the joke, tell a secret, or tell people something the subject is ashamed of or will embarrass him or her. Whether or not Freud's belief about jokes is accurate, it is appropriate to be concerned if someone is repeatedly making jokes that are particularly disturbing in nature, especially when that someone is a child.

Kim's older daughter Lisa just turning twelve when I first met her, appeared to have a habit of making disturbing jokes in my presence. At first, I didn't think much of it until she began to make these jokes on a very regular basis; almost every single time I would visit. Lisa made these jokes in casual conversation sometimes out of the blue, or at times due to specific environmental triggers, but what concerned me about her jokes is that they had to do with rape and child molestation.

Often times they would surface during roughhousing and play between the girls, Kim, and me at Kim's house. As mentioned earlier, playful aggression and roughhousing was a common occurrence with the girls. This playfulness would soon extend beyond the two of them to include both Kim and me. On several such occasions, Lisa would approach me as I sat near her mom on the sofa. She would then place her hand on my shoulder firmly and make a mock threatening statement, supposedly implying that she wanted to rape me. Kim never appeared concerned when Lisa

16

would say this to me and then soon after Lisa would usually say it to Kim as well. If the boys happened to be visiting, then they too would be recipients of Lisa's mock rape threat. Though my first instinct was to chuckle at observing this apparently silly behavior, it started to concern me with the passage of time.

Soon, Lisa would make numerous references to rape in general. If the boys or I happened to be near her, merely looking at her or engaging in horseplay, she would frequently joke that one or all of us were trying to rape her. "Don't touch or look at me, pervert!" she often said, without provocation.

There was one occasion where we had gone to a school play for one of the children, and Laura suddenly decided that she wanted to sit with me. As Laura made her way over to my chair Lisa joked to her mom by saying, "Better watch out now maybe Sumi's been raping Laura, or is likely about to begin!"

Along with many jokes using the word "rape," Lisa also made frequent jokes using the term "child molestation." There was a time when Kim, the girls, and I were eating together at a Denny's restaurant. On the restaurant window there was a banner posted which advertised that on certain nights, children could eat there for free. "We love kids!" were the words printed in big bright letters on the banner. "Ah huh, they say they *love* kids…well then they must be child molesters," Lisa said.

Yet another time I can recall, Lisa made a rather strange child molestation joke that truly stuck out in my mind. Upon discussing this with a friend later, he offered the chilling theory that perhaps Lisa was trying to tell me something through these jokes, something awful that had happened to her and that she did not know how else to open up to an adult.

Such jokes made by Lisa became even more concerning to me when she was also able to demonstrate a vast knowledge of intimate sex acts and sexual information that I felt went beyond her years. Lisa displayed this knowledge verbally, as well as through graphic drawings she often made that very accurately depicted the male genitalia. Whenever I asked Lisa where and how she had learned this sexual content, she would never give me a straight answer.

Soon, she also began to exhibit behaviors of a rather sexual nature. While the jokes, sexual talk, and drawings were things she was frequently doing when I met her, the sexual behaviors happened more after her thirteenth birthday. These consisted of engaging in extremely flirtatious conduct toward me, both verbal and physical alike. Younger sister Laura would often copy these behaviors as well, although she was only doing so to be like her older sibling. Lisa, however, was the one who had the deeper issue to deal with. In several instances, both girls would even engage in such behaviors right in their mother's immediate presence!

Remarkably, Kim did not appear all that concerned or alarmed at observing this. Rather she treated it with the same level of tamed seriousness and disapproval as she viewed the girls' habits of swearing and not cleaning up after themselves, which were also an issue. For my part, I tried to discourage the overly flirtatious behaviors by Lisa, warning her that other people may wrongfully judge her in a negative manner if they were to observe such conduct. I also warned her about how those specific behaviors may serve to draw attention toward her from males who have bad intentions.

Right along with all the sexual issues, Lisa also had significant tendencies toward aggressive behavior. There were many instances where she would lose her temper and act out quite aggressively toward me, her mother, the neighbor boys, and especially toward Laura. In most cases, it would start out as playfulness, but then escalate into something more hurtful. Often times, her hostility would include hitting, kicking, scratching, and even biting.

On one particularly bad occasion, Lisa had become enraged after Laura had grabbed the garden hose and sprayed her with water while she jumped on their trampoline. Upon chasing Laura into the house, Lisa attempted to slap her sister in the head just as I managed to step in the way. As a result, Laura was saved, but I ended up receiving the hit, and it was a really hard smack that certainly would have hurt Laura a lot! Later that evening, I got a kind text from Kim, in which she told me that Laura had said to her at bedtime, "If you and Sumi talk tonight, tell him thank you for taking a punch for me."

Though quite distressing, Lisa's concerning behaviors did not represent who she really was as a person. In reality, she was an intelligent, driven, creative, kind-hearted, beautiful young lady who I believed could do anything she put her mind toward doing, and so was little Laura for that matter. Lisa had a side to herself that was very positive, responsible, mature, and compassionate. For example, she was excellent with caring for small children and animals. On one occasion she even talked me into allowing her to bring her spoiled pet bunny inside with us at a local arcade…where both she and said bunny got plenty of attention! No matter what the occasion, I always tried to tell both girls that I was proud of them, which I truly was, as I wasn't sure how often they heard such things from their biological father.

While Lisa's concerning behaviors did not demonstrate her true personality, they did serve as a strong indicator that there were indeed deeper issues to deal with. Tragically, in spite of my best efforts, Lisa's mother Kim did not appear interested in addressing her daughter's issues. Soon there was an incident in which Lisa got into serious trouble at school for allegedly threatening other students with physical violence. Kim vented to me repeatedly about the matter consistently asserting her belief that "**I did not** raise my daughter to act this way!" At some point, I suggested to Kim that I try and find a therapist for Lisa to start seeing on a regular basis. Being that my mother is a child psychologist, I assured Kim it would be easy for my mom to use her connections and help us find someone terrific for Lisa to work with, but Kim made numerous excuses for why she felt my idea wouldn't work and eventually refused all of my offers. "I don't want some stranger knowing about my family's personal stuff!" was the reason that Kim ultimately gave for her decision.

Lisa's disturbing jokes, graphic sexual knowledge and behaviors, coupled with her aggressive tendencies and Kim's continued refusal to let her see a psychologist, all made me begin to wonder whether Kim had something to hide. Not surprisingly, I had long been concerned that perhaps Lisa had been a victim of sexual abuse. Yet when I finally confronted Lisa, she denied that she had been molested; but in spite of her verbal denial, my suspicions remained intact.

Sadly, the living conditions at Kim's home made this theory quite plausible. During the five months that I had been estranged from Kim and her girls, I once had a phone conversation with Kim's neighbor James, the husband of Joan and the father of Mark and Mike. In that conversation, James had disclosed to me that Kim had been having a number of different men over to her house following our sudden breakup. "I just saw a big, kinda scary-looking fellow going into her home the other day. She has definitely been playing the field and that concerns me for her daughters," James told me.

Kim had her own issues with rape and sexual abuse, most of which I'd learned about back when we had been dating. When Kim had been Lisa's age, she told me that an older male cousin had attempted to molest her. She also said that a male classmate had attempted to rape her during her high school years. Though Kim was careful to describe both of these incidents as being "attempts" at sexual misconduct, I wondered if she chose to minimize what had actually occurred. Then later in adulthood, Kim said a date had forced her to have sexual intercourse with him. In spite of acknowledging this violation, she still had a difficult time in labeling what happened to her as being rape. "I wouldn't really call it rape," Kim said to me back when we had discussed this. "After all, he didn't smack me around or nothing."

I responded to her by gently replying, "But he did indeed *force* you to have sex with him, Kim. So, therefore, it is rape, even if he never struck you."

Perhaps these unfortunate experiences Kim endured had influenced how she perceived rape and sexual abuse. Perhaps they had caused her to identify with the aggressor, which I've learned is not an uncommon reaction for some victims. In fact, there is an article titled, "Stockholm Syndrome and Child Sexual Abuse" by Shirley Julich, Journal of Child Sexual Abuse, 2005, Vol. 14, Issue 3, p 107-129, which goes on to state the following on this subject:

Major Indicators of Stockholm Syndrome

*The victim shows symptoms of ongoing trauma or Post-Traumatic Stress Disorder.

*The victim is bonded to the offender.

*The victim is grateful for small kindnesses shown by the offender.

*The victim denies the violence which is occurring or is able to rationalize the violence. The victim denies his or her own anger to others and to him or herself.

*The victim is hyper-vigilant to the offender's needs and attempts to keep the abuser happy. This hyper-vigilance is unidirectional, not bilateral.

*The victim views the world from the offender's perspective. She or he may not have her or his own perspective; thus the victim experiences his or her own sense of self through the offender's eyes.

*The victim sees would-be rescuers as the "bad guys" and the offender as the "good guys" or the protectors.

I soon found what appeared to be further evidence of this with Kim when I happened to learn of two male friends who she would talk about occasionally, both of whom had reportedly been convicted of sexual offenses. One was the sixteen-year-old son of a very close friend of hers, and the other was a guy she'd known back in high school and used to have a big crush on. In fact, the old high school crush was now dating one of Kim's closest friends. According to Kim, the sixteen-year-old boy was currently in juvenile detention for raping two girls, and the old crush had been found guilty in the past of raping an adult woman.

In regards to these cases, Kim would angrily vent about how she believed that both of these offenders were innocent, in spite of their convictions and that the females who accused them had supposedly, "chosen to have sex and gotten what they deserved!" Most tragic of all is the fact that I'd heard her make this damning statement in front of both of her young, impressionable daughters. At some point later, I even heard Lisa repeat the same exact statement in my presence. This, of course, concerned me greatly, as I did not want Kim's girls to wrongfully believe that most men accused of sexual offenses are innocent, and/or that most females who accuse men are usually liars who had it coming. If either of the girls were to experience an attempted or completed act of sexual abuse by a male in the future someday, God forbid, I would want them to feel as though it was okay for them to speak up and ask for help. I would never want them to wrongfully believe that something like that was their fault, as it is 'never' a victim's fault in 'any' situation! Period.

After several months of remaining single following our July 2011 breakup, Kim resumed a long distance relationship with the fellow who had previously lived with her and her girls for a three-year period. Though this man now lived in a far-away state, he would visit Kim on occasion as he still had family residing here.

Unfortunately for Kim, even this tenuous relationship would not stand the test of time. Right around Christmas 2012, Kim told me that this fellow had broken up with her, supposedly having ended things this time for good. Though she did not show it on the outside, the loss of this long-term relationship must have started to take its toll.

Yet in spite of her eagerness to remarry and to still have another child, nobody could have predicted just how far she was willing to go.

Chapter Six

A Troubling New Year's Eve Visit

Following my decision in December 2011 to keep our contact at friendship, Kim had been trying all the different dating websites out there in an ongoing effort to find 'Mr. Right'. The typical outcome would be that she had many first dates, most of which never led to a second meeting. Frequently after a date, Kim would tell me that things didn't work out because the guy was either put off by the fact that she had children, or because he had an issue with her disability. Sometimes she simply never heard back from them at all. Still, other times, she would complain that the men she met would want to use her for a sexual encounter and then nothing more.

The one thing that had kept Kim going, besides her lingering hopes of convincing me to date her again, was the on-and-off long distance relationship she'd maintained with the man who had previously lived with her for three years; but right around Christmas of 2012, that connection had broken as well.

In spite of the hardships she was privately enduring, the end of December 2012 was a fabulous time for the children and me. They, of course, had school off for winter break, and Kim had allowed me to take her girls for several days. The neighbor boys joined us, as usual, and I also invited another ten-year-old boy whom I had known through my ex-girlfriend before Kim. This boy, named Tim, had met the other four kids during the limo ride on my birthday, and they had all become friends rather quickly.

So, over winter break, I had five children in my care for three to four days. During this time, our rowdy group stayed at three different hotels, the last one simply because the heater at my house had quit working. At any rate, we had a blast, and I finally brought the kids home just a few days before the end of the year. Exhausted as I was from all the excitement and the responsibilities of managing five kids, I didn't have any big plans for the upcoming New Year's Eve.

I didn't, that is until Kim invited me to attend a gathering at her house. It was an awkward situation, as I had also subsequently been invited to come by the boys' house to celebrate with their parents. I figured I would try to make everybody happy by honoring both invitations, and I'd simply walk from one house to the other and ring in the New Year with them all.

In making her invitation through messages on Facebook, Kim had informed me that she had just been rejected by her ex-boyfriend, and was planning to have a new man attend her party as well. "His name is Rick and he's driving from forty miles out, so he'll be spending the night here for sure!" she remarked in her message. I thought it was a bit strange that Kim felt the need to inform me of this specifically, and I wondered whether or not she had some ulterior motive in mind.

As it turned out, Monday, December 31, would be a rather peculiar evening and a disturbing one as well. On the hour-long drive out to the kids' neighborhood, I kept receiving texts and calls from the girls as well as from the boys. Lisa had received an expensive new iPad for Christmas, and little Laura had also received a new electronic device with calling/texting capability.

What was happening now was that the children were fighting over me and which of their houses I was planning to stop at first. "Make SURE you come to our house first, and ONLY THEN visit the boys!" is what I kept hearing from Laura. Mark then called me moments later, and voiced his concerns over the fact that Laura had apparently told him that I was going to skip the boys' house altogether. Eventually, I was able to calm everybody down by convincing them that nobody would be shortchanged. I was happy to be friends with all of them and to share my time just as well.

Upon arriving in the kids' neighborhood, I first went to Kim's house, as per my expressed plan. As I entered her home, I immediately observed that none of the other guests had shown up for her gathering. None, that is, besides this new guy Rick, and myself. Still, there wasn't much of a chance to feel awkward, as I immediately observed an intense wrestling match between Kim and Lisa taking place on the living room carpet. Laura soon joined them in the battle, and both girls appeared extra hyper and unruly on this evening. "You missed the water fight a bit earlier," Rick then informed me, as we introduced ourselves and shook hands. He appeared to be in his mid- to upper-forties, and he came across as shy, quiet, and a little awkward. Regardless, the presence of several beer bottles told me that he and Kim had likely been drinking. Of course, that was totally expected, it was, after all, New Year's Eve.

What I did not expect, however, was to end up observing Rick taking what seemed to me an inappropriate interest in both of Kim's young daughters. During the first half hour or so that I was at Kim's house, I observed Rick making deliberate attempts to touch both Lisa and Laura, specifically playing with Lisa's ear and then playing with Laura's hair. He didn't say anything as he briefly did this, and neither girl appeared to react. I, however, was immediately uncomfortable with what I was seeing, and instinctively felt that these actions were not innocent in nature.

A short while later, Laura and I became engaged in playing a board game on the living room carpet. Rick, meanwhile, seated himself behind Laura on the sofa. Then at one point during our game, he gently caressed Laura's lower backside with his foot, just as a boyfriend would do to his girlfriend in order to be playful and flirtatious. Little Laura responded by turning around and then giggling in an awkward manner, apparently not knowing how else to react. Again Rick didn't say anything as he briefly did this. I quietly observed this interaction and felt quite uneasy with what I was seeing.

Eventually, Kim, who was also in the living room observing as this happened, led Rick down into the basement a few minutes later, presumably to smoke cigarettes. I hung around a little while longer upstairs with the girls, and then made my way over to the boys' house. I assured the anxious girls that I would spend a bit of time across the street, but then would return to their home.

Meanwhile over at the boys' house, I informed their parents, James and Joan, about the fact that no other guests had shown up to Kim's strange little gathering, besides only Rick and I. "Man, that must be pretty weird and awkward for you!" they both said in response to this info. Both James and Joan were concerned, as was I, over the fact that Kim would be letting this new fellow spend the night right away with her young daughters present in the house. "It's just not right, she shouldn't allow strange men to spend the night when her girls are around," the two of them mentioned to me.

As it turned out, the half-hour or so I spent at the boys' house watching the clock strike midnight on TV in Times Square would not be peaceful. Before long, I was bombarded with rude texts from the girls, demanding that I return immediately. Also concerned to know what was going on over there, I used these nagging messages as my excuse to get going. James and Joan said the boys could go over to Kim's with me as well, but only on condition that I would be there the entire time to look after them. "We don't trust Kim, or that man over there," they made clear to me as we left.

On our short walk across the street, Mark asked me the same question that had been on my mind the past couple of days. Exactly WHY had I been invited to this party, when and if Kim was trying to hook up with this other guy Rick? Though I didn't have an answer for him, he then went on to venture an opinion that matched what I'd been suspecting. "I think Kim has invited both you and this other man Sumi, to try and see if one of you will get jealous and attempt to compete over her."

Whatever Kim's motives had been for inviting me, the night was about to take a turn for the worse. Soon after returning to Kim's house with the boys, the four kids and I played in the living room while Kim and Rick still remained in the basement. During this period, I began to pick up on the fact that she had apparently prepared her daughters to also try and impress this Rick fellow. This became clear when one of the boys happened to say a cuss word, and little Laura angrily chewed him out by saying, "You guys 'cannot' swear here at all tonight, because mom's new friend is in the house and he don't like swearing!"

Shortly after this exchange between the children, Kim and Rick made their way back up the stairs and into the living room. Soon the wrestling match resumed between Kim and Lisa, although this time it also involved tickling, and before long they began to involve Rick in their playfulness as well.

This is where things began to get rather disturbing. At some point, thirteen-year-old Lisa began to tickle Rick's upper thigh area as he sat next to her mom on the sofa. Rick would respond to this flirtatious behavior by reluctantly attempting to chase after Lisa and/or to tickle her back, but whatever hesitance Rick may have had to begin with would disappear within a few minutes. As the boys and I observed this occurring, I began to feel sick to my stomach. I knew that many mothers in this situation would have simply told their teenage daughter to not behave in such a manner toward a strange older man.

Yet Kim, on the contrary, was the one who seemed to begin to encourage it the most! Each time the flirtatious Lisa tickled Rick's thighs, he was then egged on by none other than Kim, who sat on the sofa sipping her beer and saying, "Go ahead, Rick! Go get her! Go after her! You have my permission!" Having now been given the green light, he began chasing Lisa more freely and attempting to grab her and tickle her further. At one point, he caught Lisa and put his hands on her shoulders for several moments, as if he was fixing to give her a back rub. He then instead tickled her neck as she giggled in a flirtatious manner.

I just couldn't understand how Kim, as Lisa's mother, could possibly be comfortable with what was occurring. It was clear for me to observe from his overall demeanor that Rick was, once again, exhibiting an inappropriate interest in Lisa. Every fiber of my being wanted to stand up and tell this guy Rick to keep his hands to himself! However, with me not being Lisa's legal guardian, and with her own mother seemingly fully encouraging it, I simply didn't know how I could or should react. I also knew that if I were to voice my opinion, I would likely lose Kim's friendship for good and not see her daughters again, thereby eliminating any possibilities for the girls to communicate with me if they ever found themselves in danger.

Fortunately, these disgusting episodes were short-lived, as drunken Rick soon passed out unconscious on the sofa, and that was exactly where and how he stayed, thank God, for the remainder of my visit. He had even been passing in and out of consciousness before, but had kept being awakened by Lisa pinching at his legs.

At some point, Joan came over to the house and asked her boys to return home with her. I stayed and chatted with Kim and her girls, as Rick sat snoring loudly with his head against Kim's shoulder. He had briefly awakened once when Lisa came over to seat herself right between him and me on the sofa. I had even noticed him look at her in a somewhat expectant manner, but then close his eyes and go back to sleep after she ignored him. I also picked up on the fact that Kim appeared to be avoiding eye contact with me throughout the night. If she had indeed been hoping that we men would fight for her, that goal had not been achieved.

When I finally departed at around 3 a.m. New Year's Day, I felt pretty sure that nothing else bad would occur at their house overnight. Still, my heart ached a little as I waved goodbye to both girls, who had come up to the window to see me drive away. New Year's Eve had always been one of my least favorite holidays, and this strange little gathering over at Kim's had certainly lived up to that.

Little did I figure, on the lengthy drive home, that what happened was not all in vain. That something fortunate and positive could actually emerge from an evening as horrible as this.

Chapter Seven
Gut Instinct Proved to be Valid

If there was one positive thing that I could say about what happened on New Year's Eve at Kim's house, it's that what I observed put me on alert to be watchful for the girls' safety. The other good thing, it turned out, was that Kim did not hear from that guy Rick again. In fact, she sent me a Facebook message on January 7, to tell me that she had texted Rick about a day after the party. She said she'd told him that she and her girls had a good time with him, and she reminded him that he'd left a case of beer at her place. Kim told me she and Rick had at least six beers each that night. "Not a reply from him," she told me. "I guess the girls and I frightened him off!" Needless to say, I certainly breathed a huge sigh of relief upon hearing this, for the sake of Lisa and Laura.

Relief was not a feeling that would be around for long at all. About five days after this conversation, Kim met yet another new man and had him come over to her place on Saturday, January 12. He apparently spent the night with her, and then departed on Sunday afternoon, before the girls returned to her house from their weekend with their dad. Though I believe Kim had met this man online and they'd only had one night together, she was excitedly texting me like a teenager about how deeply in love she already was. "We had such a wonderful night together," Kim texted me. "No sex, but lots of holding one another and talking. It was truly magical. People at work are going to see me smiling tonight and will wonder what's going on with me!"

Though I was skeptical about the seriousness of Kim's feelings for this new guy, given the super short time that she'd known him, I congratulated her on having such a positive first date experience, but if there was any doubt as to just how serious she was, it was erased a mere three days later on January 16. As I was browsing on Facebook that evening, I noticed an announcement posted by Kim proudly stating that she and the new man, apparently named Charlie Jones, were now officially in a relationship. This certainly struck me as being more serious, as I couldn't recall the last time she had so quickly laid claim on any of the men she had dated. I was curious to learn more about this new man who had taken an interest in her.

Along with revealing Charlie's first and last name, Kim posted a few pictures of him on Facebook as well. I studied the photos carefully, and felt as though Charlie's smirking facial expression in one of them resembled that of a sleazy car salesman who had just sold someone a lemon. Still, there was nothing else bad or dangerous looking about him, and I tried to assure myself that he's probably a reasonable guy who wouldn't do any harm to Kim's young daughters. Besides, there wasn't a whole lot that I felt I could do about it anyway. Whether I liked it or not, this was now Kim's new boyfriend and I would have to put faith in her judgment.

Sadly, given what I knew about Kim, putting faith in *her* judgment seemed an extremely tough guideline to follow. I couldn't help having flashbacks of that guy Rick on New Year's Eve, and recalling how uncomfortable I felt in my gut when he put his hands on Kim's girls. It's sad to acknowledge that you lack faith in your friend in this regard, but it was indeed the truth of the matter. *Maybe there is something more that I could do to look out for Lisa and Laura in this situation,* I asked myself, *to try and ensure that this Charlie guy isn't going to behave just like Rick?* After much consideration, I came up with my own solution. I decided to have a full background check done on Kim's new man, Charlie Jones!

Though I knew of some basic criminal background checks that I could do by myself online, I wanted to have a real in-depth check run on Charlie to ensure the girls' safety being around him, since it appeared that he would now be dating their mother. So, I reached out to two people who I thought might be able to assist me in this process.

One was a highly respected police official of the city I lived in, who just happened to be a personal friend of mine through a prior affiliation. I also decided to reach out to my lawyer-turned-friend who had helped me in a previous legal matter.

To cover all bases, I sent out a nearly identical email to both this police official and my lawyer friend, hoping that at least one of them would be able to assist me in performing an in-depth criminal background check on Kim's new boyfriend. Interestingly, while the police official cited department regulations which prohibited him from doing such a check for me, my lawyer friend was able to do it. I found this ironic, as I'd assumed the police would be the more likely of the two to be able to help me with a criminal background matter.

Being a very proud father of a young girl himself, I guess my lawyer pal was moved by my lengthy, emotional email in which I described the whole Kim-situation to him, along with my serious concerns for her children. In fact, by the time I woke up on Thursday, January 17, he had already replied to the message I had sent him in the early morning hours. As I clicked to open his email, little did I imagine what was about to come my way; that these would be the final few moments of peace that I'd know for the next several months of my life.

Incredibly, my lawyer pal had taken just a few minutes out of his busy day to run a quick check for me on this guy Charlie Jones; amazingly, that quick check was more than enough. This is the email he sent me on the evening of Thursday, January 17, telling me what he'd discovered:

Sumi,

I quickly checked the name Charles Jones on the public records system (it's available for free to anyone online), and came up with the attached.

There are several people with that name who have various speeding tickets, but Charles Michael Jones (DOB given) was convicted of some kind of serious sex crime in 2003. Separately, he also has some child support issues in a civil matter.

This isn't a complete or comprehensive background check; there are other tools (which cost money) that can be used for that, but if this is the same guy, he definitely does have a record.

I remember being shocked and stunned as I carefully read my lawyer friend's email message. Out of all these guys he'd noted that were named Charles Jones, could it really be that my friend Kim had just begun dating the one called "Charles Michael Jones" who'd been convicted of a serious sex crime?

I would soon learn that the answer to this question was a staggering, "yes." Now having the guy's first, middle, and last name, along with his exact date of birth, I searched for him in our state's Depart of Corrections (DOC) prison website. Sure enough, I immediately came upon him. The full name and date of birth matched, and the profile contained a mugshot picture of the individual's face. Although he looked quite different and had long hair as well as facial hair in the prison mugshot photo (neither of which were present in his current Facebook pictures Kim had recently posted) I was ninety-five percent sure it was indeed the same Charlie Jones that my friend was now dating. Even worse, was when I then noted on the website that Charlie's specific sexual offense had consisted of child molestation committed upon his young stepdaughter, a female under thirteen years of age!

All of a sudden, out of the blue, I had a huge problem to deal with.

Chapter Eight
Profile of the Child Molester

Warning: The third paragraph in this chapter contains graphic descriptions of the sexual abuse of a young child. Reader discretion is advised.

Thursday, January 17, 2013, was turning out to be a night filled with revelations, each one more awful than the last. Having now confirmed that my single mom friend, Kim, the mother of Lisa and Laura, was indeed dating a convicted child molester; I quickly tried to learn everything that I could about this disturbing person.

Upon doing a Google search of his entire full name, I came upon a lengthy online report about Charlie's criminal appeals process. This report contained everything; every horrible, graphic detail concerning Charlie's sexual molestation committed upon the eleven-year-old daughter of the woman he was married to in late 2002. The report also made no small point in highlighting the overwhelming evidence against him, including the young girl's reliable testimony and his own repeated admissions to having committed the despicable crime. In fact, in the very first paragraph summarizing the report's findings, the appeals judges plainly stated, "We find the evidence easily sufficient to support the verdict of second-degree criminal sexual conduct. We affirm."

According to the report, the eleven-year-old daughter of Charlie's wife had awakened in the middle of the night on one occasion in late 2002, only to find his hand between her legs underneath her underwear, tickling her "private area" in a "bad way." The report states that the young child then rolled over in order to stop him from continuing to touch her. At that point, the report states that he then left her bedroom. It is unclear how long he had been in the girl's bedroom, fondling her genital area before the young child awakened.

Fortunately, this young child appeared to have the proper knowledge of what to do in this awful situation, along with the ability to tap into her personal reserve of courage and to take out just the right amount. According to the report, the girl neglected to tell her mother about the incident that had occurred with Charlie the morning after it happened. However, she did tell a friend at school and then eventually told her school counselor later that same day. The school counselor went on to do her job, as state law requires of her, she contacted the local police and social services to look into what the girl was saying. The report says that the authorities then interviewed her and she bravely told them the truth, just the way it had happened.

According to the report, Charlie denied the girl's allegations during his first interview with authorities, but then he began acting unusually and refusing to speak to his wife or to get out of bed, and when his concerned wife brought him to his mother's house the following day, the report states that he eventually gave in and confessed. Charlie reportedly admitted to his mother and his wife that he had fantasized about young girls, and that he had indeed entered the young child's bedroom and touched her "private area" the previous night. The report states he went on to also admit his crime again to his nurse at the psych ward of a local hospital, and later to both the cops and social services.

Furthermore, in a second interview with authorities at the hospital, the report states Charlie readily confessed to the crime and further admitted that he fantasized about young girls, specifically around the ages of twelve and thirteen. This of course concerned me greatly, as Kim's older daughter Lisa was exactly thirteen years of age! The rest of the report describes how he was convicted by a judge of second-degree criminal sexual conduct following a trial, and how the appeals court had chosen to uphold the judge's finding of guilt after a thorough review of the case.

Beyond this lengthy appeals report, I also came upon a newspaper article online which described Charlie's sentencing in 2004 by the same judge who had found him guilty. In this article, I noted that the judge had labeled him a "predatory offender" and had ordered him to officially register himself into the system as such. Along with some brief jail time and house arrest, the judge had also placed him on a lengthy twenty-five years of probation for his sexual offense, specifically stating that he have "no contact with girls younger than eighteen with the exception of his own daughter" with whom the judge would allow supervised visitation rights.

Though this sentencing, which included the brief jail term, had taken place in late summer of 2004, I found it interesting to note from the DOC website that he had actually gone to state prison for this same offense four years later in 2008! This information strongly indicated to me that Charlie had most likely gone on to violate the terms and conditions of his probation in the years after he had been sentenced. This detailed information, albeit quite disturbing, had helped me to quickly familiarize myself with the profile of the child molester.

Just as noteworthy was what I'd also learned about the absolutely devastating, crippling, long-term impact that sexual abuse can sometimes have on the victims, particularly young children like Lisa and Laura. I learned much of this from being able to utilize excellent online resources such as Stop the Silence: Stop Child Sexual Abuse – a U.S.-based international organization with a mission to expose, prevent, and stop child sexual abuse (CSA) and help survivors heal worldwide; Rape, Abuse, and Incest National Network (RAINN); and Darkness To Light, a non-profit organization in South Carolina seeking to protect children from sexual abuse. I'd read that such maltreatment can scar a child and tremendously alter their most basic self-esteem and sense of self-worth. I'd read that some child victims of sexual abuse may struggle with anger, guilt, shame, depression, nightmares, PTSD, anxiety, and other disorders or issues. I'd read how some may lose their innocence, their personal sense of security, and may struggle to love or trust others again. I'd read how some may be more likely to again be sexually abused and/or raped in the future.

In addition to all these, I'd read how sexual abuse may impact their future dating relationships in a terrible manner, possibly leading to promiscuity (having sex with many different people) and other reckless decisions which can hurt them both physically and psychologically. I'd read how some had turned to working as a sex worker, wrongfully believing because of the abuse that their only value as a human being is to provide sexual service. I'd also read how some went on to abuse alcohol and drugs in an effort to alleviate their prolonged suffering, and how in the most tragic cases, sexual abuse can lead some to suicide. Though many of the above-mentioned outcomes might not apply to the majority of CSA victims, especially those who are able to seek help and have a strong support system, these potential concerns are valid ones and one needs to keep them in mind.

Naturally, as someone who loved these girls dearly in a parental role, I wanted to protect both Lisa and Laura from all of these possible negative outcomes, especially considering the probability that Lisa may have been down this road in the past. Being a father and/or father figure to young girls, you realize there are things you will never be able to protect them from experiencing. You cannot be with them every day at school. You cannot make sure they won't fall in with the wrong crowd. You cannot prevent them from getting their hearts broken or even from being used by a manipulative, shallow jerk who is only looking for sex. You can certainly make a big difference by always being there; by listening to them; and having a loving, trusting and respectful relationship where they know they can come to you no matter what. However rarely in this life are you ever granted an opportunity where you can practically look into a crystal ball and prevent the possibility of something bad from occurring.

This situation, in particular, was one where I felt I **'could'** indeed save and protect them from any possible harm from this individual! It was a possible crime that was waiting to happen but thanks to having done the background check it was one-hundred-percent preventable now. That background check was like looking into a crystal ball, and being blessed with the chance to intervene before anything bad could occur.

Now there was only one thing left for me to do to ensure that Kim's girls would not be harmed in any way. I would have to go and warn my close friend Kim about everything I had discovered.

Chapter Nine
What to Do With What I Discovered

When it comes to awkward conversations that nobody would ever like to have in their lifetime, this one has certainly got to be within the top few. That's exactly how I felt when I began to mull over the idea of telling Kim that her brand new love was a convicted child molester! This realization only worsened when I began to imagine how she might react to receiving such devastating news from me, of all people. Though she and I had been friends now for quite a while, we had also dated briefly, and technically that made me an ex-boyfriend. Being in the ex-boyfriend category, I was concerned that she may wrongly feel I had an ulterior motive for digging up and giving her this negative information. What if Kim felt I was just doing this to ruin her new relationship out of jealously and spite, or simply because I didn't want her and her girls to be happy with somebody else?

These concerns caused me to hesitate in regard to contacting Kim right away. Instead, I brought the information I'd printed out about Charlie and drove an hour to a gas station in her neighborhood later that same evening. Once there, I phoned Kim's across the street neighbor Joan, the mother of the two boys Mark and Mike whom I'd frequently taken out for fun activities with Lisa and Laura.

Upon connecting with Joan, I asked her to drive out to the gas station and meet with me ASAP. "Oh, what's wrong? What did I do?" Joan asked me with alarm and concern. Obviously, I didn't want to meet with her at her house, which was directly across the street, in front of Kim's home. I also knew we'd have our privacy guaranteed at the gas station, given that Kim didn't drive and it was too far to walk in the winter.

Within a few minutes, Joan arrived. I quickly introduced her to my mother, whom I'd asked to come along with me as a witness. Once Joan stepped into my car, I told her my frightening discovery and I showed her the pictures I brought of Charlie. Showing her the pictures was important, as she had mentioned to me on the preceding Sunday that she had seen Charlie's face as he was brushing the snow off his car on Kim's driveway.

Without question, Joan quickly confirmed that the man in the Facebook and mug-shot photos I brought was indeed the same man she had seen the other day on Kim's driveway. To further confirm that we had the right guy, she then went on to Charlie's Facebook page on her cell phone and viewed his date of birth. Sure enough, Charlie's birth date on Facebook matched the birth date given on the prison website for one Charles Michael Jones. There was no doubt left now that it *was* indeed the same man!

From this moment forward, Joan and I became allies in our common goal to keep Lisa and Laura safe from any possible harm this convicted child molester might attempt to inflict. Joan also had a larger community interest in potentially keeping her young sons and the other neighborhood children safe from this individual as well. While I needed a day to determine how exactly I would break the bad news to Kim, Joan contacted the local police in her town and told them of the situation. Unfortunately, the officer Joan first spoke with was highly unsympathetic to her concerns and rude on top of that. However, as luck would have it, she quickly made contact with another local officer, who in turn appeared quite interested in addressing the troubling matter.

Joan and I remained in regular contact by phone over the next twenty-four hours. On the following day, Friday, January 18, Joan contacted me with what appeared to be fantastic news. She excitedly informed me that the second officer had called her back and spoken with her at length about the situation, especially addressing the stipulation that Charlie was not allowed to come into contact with female minors. "Sumi, I have good news from this police officer," Joan told me. "He says he has no sympathy for anyone who would molest children, and that he's aware of Charlie's restrictions being around female minors. He said that if Charlie were to come over to Kim's house, and if Kim's daughters are present at the time that he does, then the police can go ahead and arrest Charlie right on the spot!"

Naturally, I was quite happy and relieved to receive this update from Joan. She went on to tell me that this officer had apparently informed the other local police officers about this individual as well, and that if he were to come near Lisa and Laura, the cops should be notified immediately. Due to her presence directly across the street from Kim in the neighborhood, the responsibility of calling the police if this happened naturally fell upon Joan, and this seemed to work in my favor as she expressed feeling all psyched up to do it! Of course, both Joan and I hoped it would never come down to a dramatic arrest being made in front of Kim's young daughters. With Joan doing her part with the local police, it was now up to me to inform my friend before Charlie could ever come over.

Sumi Mukherjee

Chapter Ten

The Meeting Where It Should Have Ended

After a grueling forty-eight hours spent withering under the heavy burden of the damning information I had learned, I decided it was finally time to confront my friend with the terrible news. In spite of the risk involved with being the messenger in such a sensitive matter, I knew I wouldn't be able to live with myself if later, God forbid, something bad were to happen to Kim and her daughters, something that perhaps my informing them about Charlie could have prevented.

I also determined that in the process of doing so, I wanted both Lisa and Laura to be present during this conversation. Though Kim's neighbor had advised me to only speak with Kim in private, I felt it was essential for Lisa and Laura to learn the truth about Charlie Jones, to better ensure their own personal safety in the long-run. Since I knew that Charlie had already been to Kim's house and most likely knew many personal details about the girls, I decided that it was necessary to inform both girls in an age-appropriate manner. I remembered from when I'd first met Kim that she didn't hesitate to immediately give a new man loads of personal information about her young daughters. To assist me in the delivery of this troubling content, I requested both of my parents to come along for this difficult meeting. In addition to being witnesses to this delicate conversation, my mom is a child psychologist, and I felt she and dad would help Kim's daughters to better process the potentially frightening information. In preparing to meet with Kim and her daughters, I decided that we would

44

simply arrive at their house unannounced without prior warning. This was essential, I felt, to prevent Kim from getting a heads up about the subject matter of our conversation. If she had any idea what the conversation would be about, I was afraid that she might immediately phone Charlie and first get *his* side of the story, which I feared might consist of a rather twisted, self-serving version of what all had actually happened.

So, on the evening of Saturday, January 19, 2013, my parents and I began the hour long drive out to Kim's house to warn her and her daughters about Charlie. We went in separate vehicles, my parents in their car and me in my own, in case I ended up taking the kids somewhere or staying over afterward to comfort them. Although I had made this trip countless times now since May 2011, the same journey felt markedly different this time. This wouldn't be any ordinary visit, I realized, as I would very soon be the bearer of shocking, life-changing information.

My parents and I finally arrived at Kim's house around 9 p.m. and were readily welcomed in by a somewhat surprised mother and daughters. Kim had earlier told me that the three of them had been cleaning house and laying low that weekend, and that Laura was getting over a cold. Upon entering their home, I informed them that we had something to discuss with them of a serious nature. Having established that, Kim invited the three of us to settle comfortably into her living room. As she grabbed additional chairs from around the kitchen table for my parents to sit in, little Laura looked up at me from her rocking chair and her DS game and asked me, with all of a child's precious innocence, "Does this have to do with my pet Betta fish at your house? Did he die?"

Even at such a serious moment, a part of me had to smile at the humor involved. During one of my many days-long outings with the kids, Laura had once talked me into buying her a Betta fish to keep as a pet at my house. We had been at a Walmart store that night and she had really, really wanted it and she simply would not relent and shut up about it until I caved in and bought it.

"Oh no, honey, unfortunately this is a bit more serious than something bad happening to your fish, which it didn't," I managed to reply. Even so, the humorous part of me felt more like exclaiming, "Do you *really* think that even a true animal lover like myself would have dragged my parents all the way out here on a Saturday night over a Betta fish?!"

Having moved past Laura's grave concern for her fish, I nervously began the actual conversation. Knowing well by now how little it can take to aggravate Kim's temper and get her to become defensive, I decided not to mention that I had done the background check on Charlie solely because of what I'd observed at her house with that guy Rick on New Year's Eve.

Instead, I told Kim that I felt as though I had recognized Charlie's face from our state's prison website when I first saw the pictures she had posted of him on her Facebook. This story was quite plausible, as Kim knew I would often browse mugshots on the DOC website as part of my deep interest in criminal justice, along with the fact that we'd often watched numerous episodes of the prison television show LOCKUP together. Feeling suspicious of Charlie and concerned for her and her daughters' safety, I told her that I had my lawyer friend do the background check on Charlie. Having reached the moment of truth, I then finally told Kim and her girls that I'd learned that her man was a convicted child molester.

At first, Kim didn't have much of a reaction to my information, other than to shake her head slightly and then utter the words, "What, you think he's a child molester?!"

I told Kim that he definitely was convicted and then I pulled out and showed her all of the paperwork on Charlie; including the prison mugshot photo, lengthy appeals report, sentencing article and criminal background report that I had found on the internet. As Kim looked over the information, she soon had the exact reaction I had hoped for and well expected; she suddenly broke into tears and hugged me, burying her head in my chest. "Oh thank you, Sumi, thank you for warning me!" Kim managed to say through her sobs. I also took this opportunity to clarify for Kim that I had **'not'** dug up this information out of jealously or spite toward her being with somebody else. "Oh no, Sumi, I would never have thought that of you," she reassured me. After forty-eight hours of stressing, I felt such a huge sense of relief.

What was remarkable for me to note later, although I'd missed observing it at the time being, was the reaction that my parents observed from Kim's young daughters as their mother wept on my shoulder. Or perhaps better stated, their astonishing **lack** of any normal reaction! According to mom and dad, the girls appeared un-fazed and barely showed any hint of emotion or concern upon hearing my shocking declaration. They merely sat on their chairs and played with their pet cats and bunny, occasionally pressing the buttons on the new electronics they had each received for Christmas. "For young girls of ten and thirteen, I would have expected a lot more interest and involvement over the particular subject matter being discussed in front of them," my father later expressed to me. "I would have expected them to be wide-eyed and paying full attention, perhaps even asking you some questions about it. Yet, there was no reaction from either of them. Although they were physically present, it was as if they were not really there."

In fact, there was only one audible reaction from either one of the girls to my dramatic news about Charlie, and again it came from ten-year-old Laura. Apparently assuming as I had that their mother would now terminate her relationship with Charlie immediately, Laura looked up and suddenly stated with a profound sense of disappointment, "Oh no, now we're not going to get the new pet kitten that Charlie had promised us!" Just like that, it appeared that Charlie had already begun trying to groom Kim and these innocent children with the apparent promise of a brand new pet, although he had not even met the kids yet.

There is an excellent book that discusses this subject of "grooming" in great detail, with regards to how sexual predators

47

groom both the adult community as well as the children, which is titled "Identifying Child Molesters – Preventing Child Sexual Abuse by Recognizing the Patterns of the Offenders," written by Carla Van Dam, PhD. In her revealing book, Carla quotes a convicted child molester's description of the elaborate grooming process he would undergo long before he would molest the child. "I would obviously have met the child's family several times… I would have been invited to supper at the child's home and would have charmed the hell out of the child's parents, and they would be pleased the way their child responded to me and so obviously liked me," the offender in Carla's book is quoted saying. Convicted child molester Charlie's promise of a pet seemed to fit this description.

Meanwhile, as Kim carefully read through each chilling page of the detailed documentation, my mother engaged the girls in a productive conversation about self-defense and how they should react if an adult makes them feel uncomfortable. In between these lessons, Mom also reached out to Kim and tried to console her. Though her tone toward Kim was nurturing, my mom suggested that Kim attempt to move on and naturally terminate her contact with Charlie. "Yeah, I guess I should end it now," Kim said somewhat reluctantly. "I've only known him for one week. It's not like we've been together for a whole bunch of years."

My mom quickly backed up Kim's sentiment by adding, "He really isn't worth your tears and heartache. You certainly deserve someone far better for you, and of course for your two daughters."

At one point during our meeting, Kim began to feel the urge to call Charlie up and to angrily confront him. My parents and I strongly recommended against this. "Kim, this guy is an ex-convict who has done hard time in state prison. He's a convicted sex offender who preys on young girls, and he already knows where you and your daughters live. The last thing you want to do is to piss him off!" I told her.

Instead, I suggested that Kim send Charlie a polite text message briefly saying something such as, "I'm sorry, Charlie, but things are just not going to work out between us. I'm just not ready for a relationship after all. No hurt feelings, but I'd appreciate it if you please do not contact me anymore. Thank you kindly." All, of course, to be followed by unfriending him on Facebook. This method, I strongly felt, would likely diffuse the situation calmly without causing any bad repercussions.

As Kim mulled the idea and kept reading through Charlie's extensive paperwork, I showed thirteen-year-old Lisa exactly how to do a criminal background check on an individual, using her expensive new Christmas gift, an **iPad**. Given an individual's first and last name, along with their date of birth, I showed Lisa how to run a free check online on our state's Public Criminal History website. I then had her put in Charlie's first and last name and date of birth, and following the instructions Lisa was able to quickly access his criminal records. By teaching Lisa this, it was my hope that she would be able to run a check now herself on any new man whom Kim might meet and who might enter their lives. All in all, it seemed as though our visit had eventually come to a successful conclusion.

Or had it? Incredibly, in spite of my heartfelt, super in depth warning about Charlie's well-noted sexual deviancy toward children, it soon appeared as though my friend had other disturbing ideas. As my parents got up to leave and head back to their house, she suddenly asked me if I would be willing to take Lisa and Laura back to my place for the evening. In the time that it took me to reply that I gladly would, the excited girls were already grabbing their jackets and whatever belongings they wished to bring along with them. "What are you going to do when we leave?" I asked Kim with some caution. Sadly, she gave me the very answer that I had most dreaded to hear. "I'm going to give Charlie a call and I'm going to hear his side of the story. After all, if he's been to jail and he's paid the price, don't you think that he's learned his lesson?"

A very big part of me didn't even want to acknowledge that she had just said what she did. As a mother with two precious young daughters, I simply could not fathom how Kim could possibly be having such a reaction. After all, I had just told her and showed her, how in the world could Kim have just read through the graphic details of what Charlie did to his young victim, and now be having this reaction? What in the world had happened to her most basic maternal instinct? Both of the girls were close in age to Charlie's prior female victim, who also happened to be the daughter of the woman he had been partnered with, and both were also in the exact age range of young girls that Charlie admitted he fantasized about; but if there was one thing I knew darn well about Kim from when we had dated, it was that arguing with her and challenging her would only serve to push her further in the wrong direction. Regardless, I was surprised at how she had changed her tune shortly after my parents departed.

As troubling as this initial reaction from Kim was, I decided not to give it much worry. Instead, I rounded up the girls and then, as usual, we stopped by Joan's house and asked if the boys could also join us. Their parents said yes, and the four kids and I left their neighborhood and began heading back to my home. On our way there, we decided to stop at a nearby Walmart and do a little bit of shopping. It had been a somewhat stressful night, and I didn't mind spoiling my fun-loving kids with the typical item or two.

Just before we pulled into the Walmart parking lot, about forty-five minutes after leaving their neighborhood, I got a call on my cell phone from Kim. Within moments, my heart sank into my feet upon hearing what she had to say. Kim informed me that she'd been on the phone with Charlie from almost the moment that we'd left her place. "I've been talking with him Sumi, and it turns out it's all okay," she stunningly told me. "Charlie explained to me that he swears he had been planning on telling me all about his criminal record on our second date. He also explained that he didn't actually do what he's been convicted of having done to that little girl, and he was screwed over bad by the legal system. He

50

was unfairly railroaded, Sumi." With the kids in the car beside me, I didn't know how to respond as Kim continued to relay her flawed information. "Charlie insists that he didn't do it and I believe he's telling the truth, and I'm gonna continue to date him!" Kim declared to me over the phone.

With those dreadful words, what I thought was an end, was instead just the beginning of a nightmare.

Chapter Eleven
Attempting to Reason With Kim

Having four wonderful, super fun, and vibrant children around me at the moment was probably what helped me to keep it together in light of what Kim had just told me, and in light of the shocking turn, this evening had suddenly taken. Even so, one of the four of my young friends was able to figure out that something wasn't quite right.

Joan's now thirteen-year-old son, Mark, had hung back with me when we entered Walmart, while my other three charges had quickly scattered around the store in search of items to hoard. Of the four kids, Mark was the most perceptive and mature, and he was the one I could rely on at times to help keep the others in line.

Disturbed as I was by Kim's phone call, I soon called Joan and updated her on the troubling situation. "What, you're kidding me! She **'still'** wants to date him?!" Joan asked me with a mixture of shock and disgust. I then hid in the men's bathroom for privacy as I updated her on what all had happened, while Mark stood guard at the door to make sure none of the other kids came nearby. Eventually, Mark overheard my conversation with his mother, and promised he wouldn't say anything about it to the other children, especially not to Kim's daughters. I didn't want Lisa and Laura to know that I was in disagreement with their mother, or for them to know that she had decided to continue to date Charlie Jones.

Meanwhile, Joan and I were beside ourselves, not knowing what more we could possibly do now to keep Lisa and Laura safe from this predatory offender. "Maybe we should set up a situation where Charlie can come over to Kim's house while her daughters are there, so then we can call the police and have him arrested," Joan suggested to me as we brainstormed about it. "That would get him sent to jail and thereby force their relationship to end," she predicted.

"No way!" I replied, without hesitation as the protective father figure. "I don't want either of the girls to ever have to meet Charlie." As it turned out, we would be handed an opportunity to test Joan's suggestion much sooner than we had imagined.

On the following afternoon, Sunday, January 20, 2013 I brought the four kids back to their neighborhood after spending Saturday night at my house. I still planned to have them again for another night, as Monday the 21 was Martin Luther King Jr.'s birthday and was therefore, a day off school for the kids, but we still had to return to the neighborhood that afternoon, however, because Joan's younger son Mike had an extracurricular activity scheduled. While Mike went off to his activity the girls, Mark, and I hung out at Kim's house.

With the three kids watching TV nearby in the living room, Kim pulled me into the kitchen to have a discussion about Charlie. Once again, she began trying to assure me that Charlie was supposedly a good man, and that he hadn't really done what he'd been convicted of doing. She also kept giving him credit, like a broken record, over the fact that he'd assured her that he was *supposedly* going to tell her all about his criminal history on their second date, that is if he hadn't been exposed by me as he was. I found this argument ridiculous and absurd in the face of common sense, to put it very politely. "I mean just think about it, Sumi," she asked, "If you were a sex offender, would you really want to tell that to a woman on your very first evening with her?"

Disgusted with the question and her making such excuses for Charlie, I replied to Kim, by saying that 'I would **'never'** do anything to end up being a registered sex offender.' Having said this, she went right back into her original argument of again stating that he was proclaiming his innocence in the matter. "But he

53

admitted to it, Kim; we both read that," I told her in a soft and calm tone of voice.

Regardless of my selectively non-challenging tone, the assertion that Charlie was guilty immediately began to trigger Kim's temper. "BUT I TOLD YOU HE DIDN'T DO IT!" Kim replied with growing irritation, and she also now started to raise her voice. "Charlie *had* to admit to it, Sumi, or else they would have given him a lot more prison time and he'd still be locked up and fighting it today. That's what he explained to me. So yes, he admitted to it because he had to say that, but in reality he didn't actually do it."

Once again, I knew that her information was flawed. According to the appeals report, and in spite of his numerous confessions made to different individuals, Charlie had pleaded not guilty to two counts of second-degree criminal sexual conduct as charged in his case, and was then found guilty on both counts by a judge after a trial. Kim's implication that he had supposedly plea-bargained to a lesser charge in order to receive less prison time did not appear to hold up. With the kids beginning to hear our conversation from the open living room, I decided to keep my calm and not to challenge her any further. The volcano of her temper was already about to erupt.

Still, Kim had more to vent on the matter. Specifically, she now complained about how my mom had told her the day before to not contact Charlie again. "I can't believe she tried to tell me not to contact him ever again, Sumi. I mean, I'm thinking 'ah no, I'm in love with the guy,' I mean I've known him now for a whole week!"

Yes, I kid you not. No joke or exaggeration there. That is exactly what 36-year-old Kim said to me in her kitchen. That she had known the man for all of one week and was in love with him. I was dumbfounded beyond what words could describe. She was sounding like a teenager, and not a very mature one.

Tragically, Kim's misguided beliefs had also been reinforced by one of her closest friends, the woman who was dating a convicted rapist that Kim once had a crush on. Incredibly, this friend had assured her now that dating a sex offender supposedly did not pose a risk to her young daughters. Kim soon quoted her friend's strange view as a reason for staying with Charlie.

In an effort to calm the situation, I gently told her that I was not going to try to tell her what she should do. I made it clear that I personally wouldn't choose to take the risk of dating Charlie if I were in her place with two young daughters, but that as her friend, my duty was to inform her about him and to let her make her own decision about it. This approach seemed to calm the waters for the time being.

However, in my mind, I privately continued to brainstorm any possible ways that I could get Kim to change her decision. I typically don't make it a habit to interfere in the private lives of others, but with the personal safety of Lisa and Laura at stake, I just couldn't afford to do nothing. Those girls had blessed me with the high honor of calling me their Dad, and I was going to live up to that title.

Remarkably, within a matter of a few hours, I would be handed an opportunity to take the decision away from Kim. After Mike had finished his extracurricular activity and returned home across the street, I was planning on taking the four kids to go stay at a relatively inexpensive hotel that they had all fallen in love with. It was the same hotel we had ended up staying at unexpectedly over winter break when the heater in my house had quit working, but now they all loved the place, and so I'd promised to take them there for the night. Just as we were preparing to leave Kim's home and get going, I heard her talking on the phone with her boyfriend Charlie. "Yup, I love you too, and I'll see you soon!" I heard her cheerfully saying.

"What's that now; is Charlie coming over?" I asked, with a mixture of fear and excitement.

"Yup, he's gonna start the long drive from his place to come out here and see me," Kim replied. "You guys can even hang out here and meet him tonight, if you like."

At that very moment, I realized we might have to take Kim up on that offer.

Chapter Twelve

Misled and Let Down by the System

Just like that, all of a sudden, it seemed as though fate had served me up a golden opportunity to ensure the safety of Lisa and Laura, and without needing to get Kim's approval. With my heart pounding and adrenaline flowing in anticipation of Charlie's arrival, I quickly managed to excuse myself and stepped into the bathroom at her house. Once there, I immediately pulled out my cell phone and sent a text message to Joan. I knew I had to hurry, as the girls had a habit of using a paper clip to unlock the bathroom door and playfully barging in when I was in there. "Kim just told me that Charlie is coming over, and that he will be here in about an hour. Call the cops and let them know to be ready to come here and arrest him!" I texted Joan, "Meanwhile, I will keep the kids here until he arrives," I told her.

However, much like a movie or a sitcom, there would soon be unexpected issues that would further complicate this matter. Namely, the first snag was the fact that the kids all wanted to leave immediately and didn't want to hang around to meet Charlie. Both Lisa and Laura promptly declined their mother's invitation to meet her new boyfriend, and Mark said he was also ready to collect Mike from his house across the street and get going. Knowing that the girls *had* to be present at Kim's house in order for Charlie to be arrested upon arrival, I knew I had to come up with something, and quickly.

With the kids all being lazy in front of the TV at Kim's, I volunteered to walk across the street to Joan's house, presumably to get Mike to come over, but that was just the guise I was using.

Once at Joan's house, her family and I discussed the situation at hand and formulated a plan of action. I instructed Joan and her family that we would regrettably need to lie to the others and say that Mike had some homework he needed to finish up, and that the parents were angry at him for not doing it before his extracurricular activity. We would also tell them that Mike had to take a shower before he could leave with us. Meanwhile, I was hoping this planned delay would buy us the time we needed for Charlie to arrive at Kim's house and be taken into police custody.

With Joan's family, including young Mike, now in on the plan, I walked back over to Kim's house and broke the news to the other children. "Yeah, his parents are really upset with Mike for not finishing his homework earlier," I told Kim and the children. "They also insist that he MUST take a shower first, so we might as well hang around to meet Charlie," I explained to them all. Aside from some grumbling and complaining from all three children, none of them or Kim had any idea what was really about to happen. I was the only one at her house who knew what was soon to go down, and I remained tense and nervous as I counted down the minutes to convicted child-molester Charlie's arrival.

While Kim puttered around the house and the children kept watching the tube, Joan and I continued to secretly exchange text messages in relation to our plan. Before long, we had run into yet another snag. Joan sent me a text message saying, "I have called the cops but they are busy dealing with a major traffic accident that has recently happened nearby. They said to call them again when Charlie actually arrives, and they will try to get there as soon as possible." Being that Joan and Kim lived in a very small town, apparently, the number of available police officers was quite limited. I had assumed this wouldn't be an issue, especially since this was a Sunday night instead of a Friday or Saturday, which are generally busier nights for law enforcement, but like it or not, we would now have to deal with this accident issue as well.

I remained quite tense and nervous as we waited for Charlie. Joan and I continued secretly texting in the meanwhile. I was afraid one of the kids would become curious and ask me whom I kept messaging, but fortunately, that didn't happen, thanks largely to the entertainment provided by the Disney channel. "Make **sure** that both girls are physically inside the house when he arrives, that's crucial to the cops being able to arrest him!" Joan informed me. I now felt additional pressure and responsibility, as I would have to ensure that the kids did not go outside to play while we waited.

Amid the growing restrictions, I continued to feel as though Joan and I were operatives in the middle of some dangerous secret mission, and my heart kept pounding loudly in my chest. "Do you see him arriving, is he here yet?!" I continued to text to Joan.

"No he's not, but I'll text you the moment I see him pull up," Joan replied.

"Make sure you stay watching at the window," I texted back, "and be sure to call the cops the moment he gets here!" Yet even during such tense moments for me, all humor was not entirely lost. As we waited patiently, the kids continued to complain as to what was taking Mike so freaking long to do his homework and shower? I just shrugged my shoulders and tried to make excuses to explain such a lengthy delay.

Though it felt like an eternity, eventually I received the text from Joan saying that Charlie had arrived on Kim's driveway. "Sit politely until he walks in girls, and make a good first impression," I instructed Lisa and Laura.

Kim shot me a weird look and chuckled softly, "Sit politely girls?" Obviously, she did not know how important it was that both girls be inside the house when Charlie walked in. After coming this far, I did not want to risk ruining the chance of an arrest on some stupid technicality, such as if the girls were to step outside the house before Charlie entered first.

Mercifully, at least that did not become an issue. Within a few moments, Charlie knocked at the door and Kim eagerly welcomed him in. The children and I then had the pleasure of watching Charlie and Kim make out for several moments in the foyer. It was hard for me to comprehend that this was happening the very day after my parents and I had been over and warned her all about Charlie's criminal background. In all honesty, I had never dreamed she would see him again after that. I even recalled an incident from a few weeks ago, in which she had caught Lisa associating with adult men on an online dating website.

Lisa had apparently observed Kim doing this many times and wanted to copy her mother's behavior. When Lisa was caught she told her mom that she didn't give out any personal information, she was just messing with the minds of the men. Again I offered to help Kim get Lisa some therapy to address her need for inappropriate male attention, and again Kim declined. Kim had supposedly grounded Lisa and sternly warned her that those men she was emailing could be pedophiles, and now here Kim was, knowingly inviting a well-documented convicted child predator into her home and her children's lives. I just simply could not believe that it had actually come down to this. Here we all were, nonetheless, forced to deal with the apparent lapse in Kim's judgment.

Appearing polite, normal and friendly; Charlie made his way up the stairs and into the living room, where I then had the pleasure of having to shake the convicted child molester's hand and introduce myself. I was also polite and friendly, as I didn't want to tip Charlie or Kim off as to my real intentions. He looked different in person from the pictures Kim had posted of him on Facebook. He was about my height, 5'8", and appeared to weigh about 160 pounds, also similar to my weight. Still, there was something odd about him in general; sort of a hollow, vacant look on his face and in his eyes.

As awful as I knew Charlie to be from his criminal history, he did not outwardly come across in a creepy or inappropriate manner as did Rick. Charlie sat at the kitchen table and played cards and cuddled with Kim, and made idle conversation with the rest of us. In fact, he even offered his insight and knowledge about animals in assisting Laura and me as we played her animal guessing game on the sofa. It was one of those strange, bizarre moments in life where you have to stop and think; okay, here I am making nice and playing the animal game with a convicted child molester and registered predatory offender. Right around us sit the female children who he's possibly here for and intending to violate in the near future. **Not** an ideal situation for any of us involved!

In fact, the one thing that I ideally hoped would happen, had not yet managed to occur. Along with Mike stalling and taking his time, so too were the local police. The longer it took for them to arrive, the more I continued to worry about what all might potentially go wrong when and if they got here and attempted to arrest Charlie. What if Charlie was armed, or got violent and tried to resist arrest? Or what if he suddenly grabbed a kitchen knife and held it to one of the children's throats when they rang the doorbell? All of a sudden, I began to wonder if we were doing the right thing by setting up this risky arrest situation; but given Kim's baffling decision to continue to date Charlie and the menacing, long-term threat that this posed to her girls' personal safety, I didn't feel as though we really had any better option. Besides, I reminded myself that we were doing exactly what the authorities had advised us to do, and that we had to put our faith in the instructions given to us by law enforcement. Still, I remained very nervous continuing to ponder what could go wrong.

To date at this point in my life, the foremost wish of my entire existence was to establish my career as an author and speaker and build on the success of my first book, the autobiography about bullying and OCD, titled *A Life Interrupted*. Of course right up there with that wish, was my agonizing, heartbreaking, lifelong quest to finally, finally find and marry the right woman before I die of old age; but at that moment, waiting in Kim's living room, I was willing to sacrifice both of those wishes in exchange for merely having the cops arrive. *Oh God, **please** let the cops get here and arrest Charlie without anything horrible* *happening, that's **all** I wish for and ask for in 2013. **Please, please, please just let them get here, oh God please!** I silently pleaded.*

That prayer would not quickly be answered. Just as everyone was again becoming impatient over what was taking Mike so long to get ready, I received another text message from Joan. As you might have guessed, she did not have any good news. "Play nice in there and keep your cool," she told me. "I've called the police, but they are still tied up dealing with that accident. It will be a while before they clear out the jail and are ready for this. Whatever happens, even if you have to fake having diarrhea, make sure that you and the kids stay there until the police arrive!" Joan demanded. Regardless of this complication, it was clear to see that Joan was still 100-percent with our plan.

The children, however, were another matter entirely. "Where the **heck** is Mike?! What the **heck** is taking him soooo freakin' long?!" they continued to ask me. I so wished I could pull them aside and tell them what was really going on, so they would quit bringing up the fact that Mike was still not ready. I sure didn't want Charlie and Kim to figure out something was up.

As the kids waited for Mike and I continued to wait for the cops, Charlie began chatting with the children about his pet cat and his impressive knowledge of video games. The kids all began to interact with him, including Joan's son Mark, who started asking Charlie questions about certain games. Once again, I believed this to be the grooming process of a calculating child predator, and it appeared as though the kids were beginning to look at him as a pretty nice fella.

Carla Van Dam's book, *Identifying Child Molesters* makes note of how offenders often take great pride in how clever they were to manipulate everyone. As one molester in the book pointed out, "When a person like myself wants to obtain access to a child, you don't just go up and get the child and sexually molest the child. There's a process of obtaining the child's friendship, and in my case, also obtaining the family's friendship and their trust.

When you get their trust, that's when the child becomes vulnerable and you can molest the child."

In spite of the serious nature of the situation at hand, some humor was still to be found. Back at Joan's house, poor little Mike was taking what was now turning into a forty-five-minute shower! At one point he'd finally gotten out, but was told by Joan to run back in when an impatient Mark popped over to see what was taking so long.

At long last, probably an hour after Charlie had arrived, a police officer finally showed up at Kim's house. "The cops are here!" Joan texted me as I quietly breathed a huge sigh of relief. "One is sitting in his car outside and the other is walking up the driveway," she informed me.

That officer knocked on the door. "It must be Mike at last," I said in order to keep up the cover.

"Ah no, it's actually a police officer," Mark said as he went to the door.

Fortunately, my concerns about Charlie responding violently did not come to pass. On the contrary, he barely seemed bothered at all over this development. "Your neighbors must've called 'em," Charlie said to Kim in a totally nonchalant manner as they both got up to answer the door. I had told Kim the day before about how I'd informed her neighbor Joan on January 17 about her dating Charlie, so Kim must have told him that and he was now assuming correctly that Joan had called the police. What Charlie and Kim didn't yet suspect, of course, was my involvement in the whole matter. Upon entering Kim's house, the officer asked Kim and Charlie to step into the basement with him, away from the children and me, to have a private conversation. Once again, Lisa and Laura appeared unfazed in light of this unusual occurrence.

As it turned out, the visit from law enforcement would last for another long hour. All that while, I sat on the couch and texted back and forth with Joan, as the children watched TV calmly and played on their electronics. Throughout this hour, I was able to hear just bits and pieces of the conversation that was happening in the basement. At one point, I heard Charlie begin to walk back up the basement stairs, only to be firmly told by the officer, "Oh no, you need to stay down here, sir!" A while later, I heard Charlie explaining to the officer about how he had supposedly undergone sex offender treatment with success. I then heard Charlie making the point to the officer that Lisa and Laura were both old enough, in his opinion, that they could call for help if they felt threatened while Charlie was at their home. Still later, I heard the officer call a colleague on his cell phone and appear to be asking the colleague for advice as to what should be done in this situation.

"Let's just cross our fingers and hope for an arrest," Joan texted me on my cell phone.

Yet tragically, after all of our tremendous effort, distress, and hassle, no arrest was made on this evening. This was a devastating setback for Joan and I, especially given the guarantee she had received from law enforcement that Charlie would indeed be arrested if the girls were present when he visited. Instead, Kim finally emerged from her basement and said to me angrily while pointing in the direction of Joan's house, "That Joan called the cops on us!"

While the officer continued to talk with Charlie in the basement, Kim then had a word in front of me with her confused younger daughter Laura. "What happened sweetie, is that Charlie won't be able to spend an overnight here until one year from now, because of what's on his criminal record," she explained to Laura softly on the staircase. I winced inside at the stunning implication in her statement; meaning that after one year's time Kim would readily welcome Charlie to spend overnights with her daughters at home. I recalled that he had committed his previous crime overnight, when that little girl's mother was naturally asleep and unable to protect her young daughter. I shuddered at the thought that the same thing, or worse, could happen to Lisa and Laura.

Soon after observing this conversation, the kids and I finally collected Mike and we headed out to the hotel near my house where they were all dying to stay. There happened to be a 24-hour restaurant right across the street from the hotel, and there I was able to talk with Joan in private about what all had happened.

"Sumi, after you guys left, the officer stopped by and told me everything that occurred when he spoke to Kim and Charlie," she said. "He told me that he had talked to both of them together, as well as also separately, and that he had fully explained to Kim just exactly what Charlie had been convicted of doing." Joan then paused and continued by saying, "The officer then explained to me that Charlie is NOT permitted to spend an overnight at Kim's house if her daughters are also present underneath the same roof. He is also NOT permitted to be alone with the daughters at all, so that if Kim were to use the bathroom, Charlie would be required to step outside her house and wait outside until she was done and out of the bathroom."

While it was good to know that the local police had enforced some restrictions, Joan and I both felt as though we had not achieved our main objective. I also felt extremely confused by what had occurred, as Charlie's sentencing report had clearly stated "No contact with girls younger than 18." Had the confused officer made a mistake in not arresting Charlie, or was that report somehow incorrect? In either case, Joan and I strongly felt misled and let down by the system, but even though our desired result went unachieved, the two of us had certainly succeeded in angering Charlie and Kim.

Before very long, I would have to deal with the consequences of that.

Chapter Thirteen
Pursuing Alternative Methods

In spite of the ongoing situation with Charlie, the kids and I had a good time at the hotel. Between ordering movies, prank calling each other's rooms, and raiding the snack machines, we were able to take our minds off what had occurred. Amid our joyful activity, it was easy for me to not dwell on the fact that Charlie was back at Kim's house.

Easy that is, until waking up the next morning. As I rose on Monday, January 21, I decided to send Kim a polite text message to say hello and confirm what time she wanted the girls to be home that evening. Though the kids had the day off for Martin Luther King Jr. Day, I would have to bring them all home that night for school the next morning. In response to my text, Kim replied by saying that she and Charlie were doing well, and that I should bring the girls back by about 8 p.m. However, after confirming the return time, Kim then sent me a more challenging text at 12:17 p.m. plainly stating, "You could have told me what you and Joan had up your sleeves last night, though I knew something was up… Mike to do homework on a Saturday night and take that long?"

I swallowed hard upon reading Kim's text as I knew it was time to face the music. In response, I replied by reminding her that last night had actually been a Sunday, and by asserting that I hadn't had anything up my sleeve with Joan. Not satisfied, Kim responded by angrily replying, "You could have told your friend Joan to stop and didn't have to hide what she was up to!" In response to this second fiery text, I continued to deny knowing anything about last night's call to the cops. Though Kim declined to respond after this, the issue was far from resolved.

In fact, she and I would end up having a lengthy discussion about this when I brought her girls home that evening. Tragically, she made sure the conversation took place right in the girls' immediate presence. Standing together in Kim's foyer, with Lisa seated on the stairs and Laura sitting on the floor, she explained to me her reasoning for continuing to date Charlie. "Remember those two male friends of mine who were convicted of rape but were actually innocent? Well, Sumi, that is exactly what has happened here again with Charlie," she attempted to enlighten me. "He told me that the little girl was a liar and changed her story many times about where he had supposedly touched her, and that the girl's mother was an unreliable drunken woman who cannot be trusted. Charlie is a father himself with a daughter of his own, so therefore I don't believe he would have done anything to this other little girl who was a known liar." In trying to make her case, she then informed me that Charlie's probation officer (PO) was supposedly on his side in all matters, and that his PO supposedly believed in him.

The only thing that stopped me from arguing again with Kim at this moment was that I knew I would lose her friendship and never get to see her girls if I showed any signs of disapproval, and that would make it very difficult for me to be there to protect the girls. Once again I knew that her information from Charlie was flawed, as it clearly stated in the appeals report that his young victim had never changed her story about what he had done to her, but I didn't want to argue with Kim in front of the girls. Instead, I nodded silently in acknowledgment of what she was telling me, but did not verbally voice any agreement with it. I hated that she had opened this conversation in front of her daughters, and wondered how utterly confused they must feel over hearing her twisted version of the truth. I hoped that they'd be able to sense that their mother wasn't correct.

At any rate, Kim must have been able to sense my unspoken disapproval. Soon I would learn that my fears of losing Kim's friendship over this matter were not unfounded. Little did I know it right then, but that evening would be the last time that I'd get to see Lisa and Laura.

It would not, however, be the last time I would hear from them. Just six days later, on Sunday, January 27, I received an angry text message from little Laura at 8:59 p.m. "You suck!!!!!" was the exact contents of the stunning message she sent me.

Confused, I immediately replied to Laura's text by asking her, "Why? What did I do?"

The child then responded tersely by replying, "You ruined my mother and Charlie!"

Soon after this, I also received a text message from Kim. In her message, she explained to me that someone unknown had apparently contacted Kim's parents as well as her ex-husband Dave's brother, and had reportedly sent them all a letter telling them about Kim's involvement with Charlie and the recent visit from the local police. Suspecting that her old enemy Joan and/or I were behind these letters, Kim criticized me in anger for having told Joan about Charlie. "True friends mention personal stuff, anything, to friends before getting others involved," she vented. "Don't bother texting my girls."

Kim and I would go on to have many further conversations about this issue, all via emails and texting, and her complaint remained with the fact that I had informed Joan about my findings regarding Charlie's criminal history on Thursday, Jan. 17, two days before I told Kim anything about it. I repeatedly explained to her that I felt I had to inform Joan first because I knew that Joan had seen Charlie previously on Kim's driveway and that she could confirm for me that it was indeed the same man as in the mugshot picture. I tried explaining to her that I had naturally sought to obtain full confirmation about his identity first, prior to disrupting her life with the troubling information.

Regardless of who had sent the anonymous letters, it was a significant setback for Kim that her parents now knew about Charlie, as she was heavily dependent upon her folks (due to being legally blind and unable to drive a car) for all of her and her daughters' transportation needs. Kim had previously implied to me that if her parents were to learn about her relationship with Charlie, they would stop driving her to work and providing the transportation, and from messages that I soon observed on her Facebook, it appeared as though her folks had now ordered her to quit seeing Charlie, or else they would no longer continue to drive her. Therefore, it was by informing Joan, in Kim's opinion that I had managed to "ruin" plans for her and her boyfriend. Kim's anger about this was one thing, but I felt it was extremely immature and low of her to turn little Laura against me.

Yet in Kim's view, she still hadn't done enough to get even. Feeling a vengeful need to retaliate further, she soon sent me a barrage of angry text messages and emails, calling me a jerk and sarcastically thanking me for telling Joan about Charlie. When I declined to respond to these, she then escalated her behavior by threatening to find ways to end my friendship with her neighbors. Before long, Kim followed through with this threat, and sent Joan a text message revealing some of my silly antics (i.e., practical jokes) around the children. Ironically, Kim had been present herself during many of these. James and Joan were both very forgiving toward me since they quickly realized that no malice was intended. Although I never had bad intentions, this served as a good lesson and reminder to me that an adult must always monitor their conduct around children and cannot get carried away, especially in the role of a Father Figure.

Whatever feelings of relief I may have experienced upon learning about the breakup of Charlie and Kim would not be around for long. As the following week progressed, I soon saw strong indications on Facebook that the pair were planning to resume their romantic relationship, in spite of Kim's parents' disapproval. Along with expressing their love in messages to one another, I observed Kim promising Charlie that she was going to make little Laura send him a special card for Valentine's Day. This information left me disgusted beyond words. It was one thing for Kim, as a grown adult, to knowingly choose to date a convicted child molester and noted predator of young girls, but to apparently encourage her ten-year-old daughter to connect with him was perverse on a much higher level!

Furthermore, I was also troubled by something that Kim had mentioned to me on Saturday, January 19 when I had informed her about Charlie's criminal history. I recalled Kim had said back then that she had been planning on taking the girls and spending several days at Charlie's house, over the next weekend that the girls would be in her care, which would now be that upcoming weekend. Seeing how Charlie and Kim appeared to be resuming their courtship, I quickly became concerned that she might follow through with this plan.

Determined to protect Lisa and Laura, I informed Joan about Kim's intended plan for the weekend, and together, Joan and I immediately sprang into action. For her part, Joan took it upon herself to contact Charlie's PO and inform him about our concerns. She told me that the PO listened to her intently, and commented that he might make a surprise visit to Charlie's house over the weekend, to ensure that no female minors were present.

For my part, I decided to send a follow-up email to my friend in law enforcement, that police official in my city whom I had known through a prior affiliation. I sent him a lengthy message on Wednesday, January 30, and he sent a reply to me later that same day.

In his message, my cop friend heavily applauded my efforts to protect the girls in doing the background check and then informing the cops in Kim's city. He remained puzzled as I did, however, as to why the police did not take a more aggressive approach and arrest Charlie on January 20. "If he is a Predatory Offender and has restrictions that are stipulated in our State system, why are the local law enforcement officials not taking action?" he inquired. "They would be compelled to do so and if they choose not to, I would consider calling the Bureau of Criminal Apprehension (BCA) who governs the Predatory Offenders Program."

Along with this strong endorsement, my cop friend encouraged Joan and me to put pressure on the local police to take further action, and to ask them for greater clarification as to why no arrest was made. Over the next two days, I sent my cop friend more information about Charlie's criminal record and my concerns about the upcoming weekend. In response, he offered to personally contact the local sheriff in Kim's city and speak with him directly about the matter.

While it seemed as though some things were moving in a positive direction, my concerns and suspicions continued to mount. Also, on Wednesday, Kim suddenly unfriended Joan, Joan's entire family, and me from her Facebook. This move worried Joan and me greatly, as we began to wonder what information Kim was now attempting to conceal from us. Naturally, this only served to strengthen our belief that she was going to make plans with Charlie.

Following the advice of my friend in law enforcement, Joan spoke again with the same local officer who had earlier told her that he has no sympathy for anyone who would molest children. Only now, for some reason, this officer appeared to be changing his tune in the matter. "Back off, you are pushing the envelope!" is what he sternly warned her. Joan and I were both rather puzzled as to what had suddenly changed his demeanor. It was a mystery and yet another snag in this already frustrating case.

Luckily for Lisa and Laura, neither Joan nor I was about to give up on ensuring their personal safety. After further discussions between us, we decided that she should go ahead and inform the girls' father's side of the family about what all was occurring. Along with informing law enforcement, Joan and I hoped that alerting more relatives about the risks these girls were facing would ultimately put more pressure on Kim to end her contact with Charlie.

Joan also felt it would be best to approach the extended family, instead of going and informing Lisa and Laura's father directly. Joan then explained to me that the girls' father, named Dave, has a significant learning disability, and is unable to read at more than a third-grade level. Because of his disability and other issues, his mother Kathy often looked after him. Joan felt it would be safest to approach Dave's brother first, and let him relay the information back to Kathy. Dave would then be able to find out through her. Fortunately, Joan had a prior friendly relationship with Dave and his family members, dating back to when he was married to Kim, and had also been Joan's neighbor. So on Thursday, January 31, Joan met with Dave's brother and told him all about Kim dating Charlie. Joan also left the paperwork I had dug up on Charlie's criminal record, and he said he would forward the information to his mother once she got back into town.

Our decision to inform these family members led to some revelations for me regarding Dave. Though Joan confessed that Dave was by no means an angel, she went on to tell me that he was nowhere nearly as bad as I was originally made to believe. Joan told me that during the girls' younger years, it was their father who would always be out in the yard and playing with them, while their mother kept to herself and remained inside the house. To summarize his overall character, Joan referred to Dave as being someone like the famous movie character Forest Gump; a simple, happy-go-lucky kind of guy with his fair share of flaws (in Dave's case) but also with a good heart underneath. "Dave was a real easy going guy, Sumi," Joan continued to explain to me. "I even remember how he would walk across the street and ask me to read his mail to him because he wasn't able to read it himself." With this modified image of Dave, I became more hopeful that he and his mother would take some interest and protect the two girls.

Tragically, my police official friend was unable to contact the sheriff in Kim's city before the end of the business week on February 1. As a result, I remained on pins and needles as to what was going to happen to Lisa and Laura over the weekend. Joan was also quite concerned about this, and said that she would keep an eye on Kim's house. Though I generally remained stressed all through Friday evening, I had finally begun to relax a bit around 1 a.m. early Saturday morning. In fact, I had decided to go visit a good friend of mine on his lunch break at a local Walmart store, where he worked as a member on the overnight crew.

Just as I began the half hour drive to go see him, I suddenly got a call on my cell phone from Joan. "Sumi, I've got really bad news!" Joan informed me with great concern. "There was a short period of time where I had to leave the neighborhood and go run some errands." she told me, "but since I got back after 9 p.m. I don't see any sign of Kim and the girls over at their house, and everything's pitch dark over there." I immediately felt my heart stop in my chest as I continued to listen to her. "What's worse, Sumi, is that I see a fresh pair of tire tracks in the snow leading up to Kim's garage door and then stopping. I think Charlie came and took them somewhere, Sumi, and I don't know where they might be by now."

Upon receiving this information, I knew I wasn't going to see my friend anymore. All I could think was to imagine that Kim's poor girls might be with that man, and the very thing that I had dreaded all week was finally coming to pass.

Chapter Fourteen
The Worst Ever Possible Weekend

Terror filled my heart on the early morning of Saturday, February 2, 2013, as I drove down a lonely stretch of road in the middle of the night with a feeling of dread unlike any other I had ever experienced. After pulling onto an exit ramp and turning my car around, I phoned my friend working the overnight shift at Walmart. I told him an emergency had occurred, and that I wouldn't be able to meet with him. Now heading back toward my house, I reconnected with Joan and we continued to discuss the dire situation. It was hard for me to think clearly, as my mind was flooded with thoughts of what Charlie might do to the girls.

Part of me wanted to scream at Joan for having taken her eyes off Kim's house even for a split second, but I knew that she wasn't responsible for whatever had occurred. Instead of being destructive and panicked, I knew I had to come up with yet another new plan of action. In order to do so, I first had to ask myself that if I was Charlie and I had Kim and her girls in my car, where would I choose to take them?

Though it was entirely possible that he had brought them all the way back to his house, my gut told me that probably wasn't the case. I knew that Charlie's home was about an hour and a half drive away from Kim's, and felt it was not likely that he would've picked them up and then driven them all the way back. Instead, I suspected that Charlie and Kim may have decided to stay at a nearby hotel with the girls, so as to escape the watchful eye of her neighbor.

With this thought in mind, I requested Joan to drive by the nearest hotels (the hotels closest to Joan and Kim's neighborhood) and to check their parking lots for Charlie's vehicle. Joan and I both knew the make and model of Charlie's car, as well as the license plate number, from when he had come to Kim's house on January 20. Though it was after one o'clock in the morning, Joan agreed to drive by two area hotels and look for his car. Since the police had stated that Charlie was **not** permitted to spend an overnight in the presence of Lisa and Laura, I felt that catching him in the act would ensure his arrest this time around. I urged Joan to investigate further and to call 911 if she were to see Charlie's car in the parking lot of a nearby hotel.

Meanwhile, after reaching my house, I jumped on the computer and looked up the non-emergency phone number for the police department in the city where Charlie lived. Upon finding it, I called the number and spoke with the officer who answered the phone. Not wishing to experience retaliation from Kim and Charlie, I asked if I could please remain anonymous and not reveal my name in reporting my concern. When the officer assured me that I could remain anonymous, I reported my concern about the possibility that convicted child molester Charlie Jones might indeed have Kim and her girls over at his house for the weekend. I told the officer all about Charlie's restrictions being around female minors, especially in regards to overnights, as well as how worried I was about the safety of Lisa and Laura. I also provided the officer with two different home addresses I was able to find for Charlie, as well as the address of his mother's house just in case he had taken them there.

As the cop noted down all of my information, I also gave her the contact info for Charlie's PO. She then assured me that she would pass this report along to the officers out on patrol in that county, as well as send an email to Charlie's PO making him aware of the situation.

Having done all this, I then heard back from Joan that she was unable to spot Charlie's car at any of the area hotels. Though she and I had done everything that we could possibly think of, I couldn't relax as I wondered where Kim and her daughters could be. There were still possibilities that we couldn't cover, such as if Charlie had taken them to a hotel near his house, in which case the cops would not be able to find him at the addresses I had provided. Not knowing where they were left me with a feeling unlike any other. It was such a sinking feeling in the pit of my stomach; a helplessness so awful I couldn't focus on anything else. Soon, I couldn't help but wonder if Charlie were with them somewhere, right at this very moment, how long would he wait before possibly making a move on the girls? How would Lisa respond if he were to make sexual advances toward her? Or how would little Laura react if he were to come after her?

These thoughts made me shudder, accompanied by the knowledge that Kim may not take actions to discourage such behavior. The thoughts kept tormenting me without mercy; is he touching them now? Or how about now? Are they scared and in tears? Are they wishing I was there to help them? It was torture to not know what was occurring, or whether Kim's daughters were safe. As a father figure, and with kids growing faster nowadays, you naturally worry to some extent about the possibility of the girls you care about becoming pregnant at an early age, but never should you have to worry, that they might become pregnant by their mother's boyfriend! Yet, knowing Charlie's record and his voiced fantasies, I felt this was a valid concern.

As you can probably imagine, it was difficult for me to get a lot of quality sleep overnight. Upon waking up late Saturday afternoon, I had a quick meal and then met up with a young boy who I was mentoring through the Big Brothers program in my city, and as usual, spending time with a fun child helped to take my mind off my troubles. We ended up going to a popular mall that evening and watching a movie together. We then stopped at the mall arcade afterward to play several games that he liked.

It was at this point in the day that I happened to hear from my friend Joan again, and as per our regular pattern of contact, she did not have any good news. "Sumi, I have noticed that Kim and her girls are at their house after all, and that they most likely spent last night there as well," she informed me. "However, I still believe that the tire tracks I observed in the snow on Kim's driveway last night were evidence of Charlie's arrival. I'm willing to bet that his car is in her garage, Sumi, and that he spent the night at her house with her daughters present!"

Troubling as this news was, I now saw a fresh opportunity for us to help get Charlie arrested. However, this could only happen, if we were able to PROVE that Charlie had spent the past night at Kim's house. Thinking the same thing as I was, Joan said she was planning to walk into Kim's yard and look through the window at the back of her garage, to check for certain if Charlie's vehicle was inside. I strongly encouraged Joan to go do this, and waited tensely until I heard back.

Sure enough, Joan called me back several minutes later and confirmed that Charlie's car was indeed inside the garage. "Yes, this time we got him!" I proclaimed with excitement. I then called the police department I had spoken with last night, in Charlie's city, and informed them of this new development. They said it would take them some time, but that they would follow up on my tip.

If there was any need for more clarification as to Charlie's presence, it would soon be forthcoming. Just as I was dropping off the child I was mentoring at his house, I heard back again from Joan. This time, she informed me that she had recently observed Charlie pulling out of Kim's garage with her and both girls in his vehicle. They had disappeared for a short while, but then Joan observed them all returning together. "I saw it for myself now, Sumi!" Joan informed me. "Charlie was in the car with Kim, and I saw both girls getting out of the car as well. They are all at Kim's house together right now, and I'm sure that he spent the night."

Joan's eyewitness account gave me everything I needed to take further action. Armed with this information, I then called the police department in Kim's city and told them everything about what was occurring. Having Joan's permission, I gave them her name as being the eyewitness to all of these recent events. Though the officer answering my call told me they would respond to my concern, she seemed to be more disturbed over the fact that Joan had walked into Kim's backyard. "You should warn your friend Joan that what she did is trespassing, and that she can be charged with a crime herself," this lady told me.

Okay, let me get this straight. Here we have a convicted, registered child predator spending an overnight illegally; according to the records, near vulnerable female minors. The guy committed his previous sex crime against a young female child overnight, and admitted that he fantasized about young girls. He's been to jail for it, violated his probation, was then sent to state prison and this cop is worried about Joan walking in her neighbor's backyard? I could hardly believe what I was hearing.

Having placed a call to the police in Kim's town, the wheels of justice appeared to be turning. Joan soon contacted me and revealed that the local cops had spoken to her, and that they asked her for confirmation that Kim's girls were near this offender. Once Joan had confirmed it, they then told her that they would work on obtaining a warrant for Charlie. As fate would have it, the officer who contacted her happened to be the same one who had recently told her that he felt she was "pushing the envelope" with her involvement in this matter. So in turn, this officer made sure to chew Joan out for her decision to walk in Kim's yard. "That officer really let me have it, Sumi!" Joan told me. I assured her that I still felt she'd done the right thing, for the sake of Lisa and Laura. Knowing Charlie had spent the night at their house totally gave me the creeps. While Joan and I waited for the police to act, she phoned the brother of the girls' father, Dave, and gave him an update as well.

Finally, around 10:30 p.m. Saturday night, the police arrived at Kim's house. Joan informed me by phone as this was occurring, as I held my breath and prayed for an arrest. "There are three officers walking up the driveway this time," she told me. Within moments, the officers had entered Kim's house, and would not step out for several more minutes.

Then at last, to our utter shock and dismay, Joan reported to me that the officers had left Kim's house without taking any action. Without taking any action, that is, besides the fact that they then apparently came over to Joan's house and chewed her out yet again. "Oh boy, an officer is yelling at Joan right now and he's really pissed!" was the report I got from a friend of Joan's named Michelle, who was also at her house and had taken charge of the phone. "The officer is yelling at her, Sumi, and threatening to press charges against her if she calls them again about this concern."

Sadly, this would not be the only rage poor Joan would encounter on this dreadful evening. Moments after the cops chewed her out, she received a scathing verbal attack from disgruntled Kim. "You better back off and leave us alone!" Kim yelled at her over the telephone. "Charlie is my boyfriend and he'll be here every weekend, so you better just learn to back off!"

After all the smoke had cleared, I finally heard back from her. Sobbing and in tears, a broken Joan told me everything that had occurred. "I am done with this, Sumi, I tell you **I am done!**" is what my friend and number one ally was now saying. "I have done all I can and the police are allowing Charlie to stay there, so there's nothing more I can do for those girls."

I felt for Joan and was stunned over what was occurring. Never had I heard of an officer saying to NOT call them about a concern, and/or then threatening to press charges against a citizen for doing so. Why in the world had the police allowed Charlie to stay there, and why were they having such an unprecedented negative reaction? Joan might have had enough of this fight, but I wasn't about to give up.

Whatever the reasons behind it, I knew in my heart that what happened that night wasn't right. After consoling Joan and allowing her to take a breather, I called the local police department in my city and asked the responding officer if he could possibly contact my friend, the same police official who had strongly encouraged Joan and me to push forward. Although this officer was unable to do that, he did take the trouble to contact the cops in Kim's town and confront them yet again about the issue. However, after having done so, he gave me an answer that was less than satisfactory. "I have spoken with those fellow officers in your friend Kim's town, and they have assured me that everything that needs to be done is apparently being done correctly in regard to this situation."

Seeking further clarification, I then asked the officer if this meant that Charlie was legally allowed to spend overnights near the children. In a response that only deepened my confusion, the officer replied by saying, "No, he is **'not'** allowed to spend overnights at the residence."

At this moment in time, I simply did not know what to think anymore, as Charlie had, of course, spent the previous night there! As distraught, confused and defeated as I felt; I forced myself to keep moving forward. I sat down and sent a very long email explaining everything that happened to my police official friend, intending for him to read it when he got to work on Monday, but after completing that task, all I could do was sit there and wonder what might happen to Kim's poor girls overnight.

It was unbearable knowing that Charlie was with them at that time, and there was nothing under the sun that I could possibly do about it. I had now called the police in three separate counties; Charlie's city, Kim's city, and my city; and they had all failed to take what I thought would be appropriate action. Never in my life had I felt such an overwhelming sense of helplessness. Little Laura's bedroom was right next to her mother's, where I knew the convicted child molester who fantasized about young girls, would likely be spending another night. Is he touching them now? Is he touching them now? Is he touching them now? That was the only thought that kept funneling through my mind, as I had run out of available options to ensure their personal safety. This was for sure, without any doubt, the worst ever possible weekend.

That is not to say, of course, that there wasn't still one more thing to come. At exactly 1:43 a.m. on Sunday, February 3, 2013, I received the following email message from my former friend Kim:

"I owe you an apology some what... found out tonight who the culprit is that is creating hassles. Police came over tonight as Charlie, girls, and I were playing a game of Sorry. Charlie and I did not get in trouble what so ever... instead, police looked into Charlie and I's eyes and said that we should get a restraining order on neighbor lady whom you are still friends with. You can possibly get my trust back, if you can promise me that you will no longer associate with my neighbors. Period."

Chapter Fifteen

Guidance From a Guardian Angel

While I might have hoped that the disastrous weekend would give way to a better start of the new week, I would soon find I was still out of luck. Although Kim had recently unfriended Joan and me from her Facebook, we had discovered that we could still see some communication between Kim and Charlie by periodically viewing Charlie's Facebook page, and in doing so on Monday, February 4, I came upon an awful discovery. Kim had followed through with making little Laura send Charlie a special card for Valentine's Day. Posted nicely on his Facebook page, was a crayon colored picture of a brown dog wagging its tail joyfully with a big red-colored heart displayed on its chest. Written in blue crayon, were the words, "To Charlie From Laura. Happy Valentines!"

At the bottom of the posting was Charlie's grateful response to the young child, saying "My first Valentine this year. Thanks, Laura."

Naturally, this disturbing post made me even more eager to touch base with my friend in law enforcement, who I hoped had received my lengthy email message regarding what all occurred over the weekend. As it turned out, I would indeed hear from my cop friend later Monday afternoon. However, my run of bad luck would continue, as my cop friend too now appeared to have changed his view on this matter:

Sumi:

I am sorry that we did not connect over the weekend when you sent some of your messages to me, but I wanted to let you know that I spoke directly with the sheriff in Kim's town today. He was aware of the case and advised for me to send him the information that you provided initially to me. I also explained that you and the neighbor in question wanted to keep any personal identifying information private. As I explained, their sheriff's office will determine whether or not that can happen based on the case's circumstances.

From this point on, I need you to directly communicate with their sheriff's office on this matter. It is not appropriate for me to be in the middle as I do not have jurisdiction in this case and do not know all of the facts.

Please follow what you are told by their sheriff's office. I know that you have great concerns for the children's welfare, which is noble and right, but let the officials review and investigate. Lastly, if you want to contact Child Protective Services (CPS) that is an option, but know that the Sheriff's Office works closely with them and most likely has them involved if warranted.

Though I believe that my cop friend meant well, I was confused since this was not in line with the confidence and determination he had previously displayed. Not only had he now prohibited me from contacting him any further on this matter, but he had also excused himself from this situation without following through and reporting our concerns to the BCA that governs the Predatory Offenders Program.

Following this latest discouraging setback, I began to feel as though I had exhausted all possible forms of intervention. Joan was no longer on board with these efforts, and my only supporter with law enforcement ties was not able to help anymore.

As it turned out, I never did hear any word back from the sheriff's office in Kim's city. Yet, there was something deep down inside of me that still refused to give up. From the start, this whole thing had been about trusting my gut instincts, and my gut was telling me **'This is not right and there has got to be more I can do!'** While it certainly seemed like a lost cause, I continued to brainstorm for new ideas.

Feeling like I was in crisis mode, I suddenly got the idea to try contacting a sexual assault crisis counselor. I figured I was at ground zero and had nothing left to lose, and perhaps placing a call to a crisis hotline might give me a new idea I had not yet considered. At any rate, I felt it would be a place where I could at least vent to someone who was likely to sympathize, and to whom a call regarding this delicate matter would be an appropriate move. Between February 4 and 5, I did a Google search for a 24-hour rape/sexual assault crisis phone hotline and came upon one in a nearby city. Upon finding the number online, I called it during the overnight hours and was transferred by the operator to a trained crisis counselor.

The counselor who took my crisis call that night was named Betty, and the sound of her voice immediately made me feel as though I was speaking to someone who cared. She had a very gentle manner about her, and the more I openly shared with her the more concerned she became about my unique dilemma. With the lack of support from the children's mother, along with the recent loss of support from Joan and my friend in law enforcement, I needed someone in power to step up and tell me that they too saw important purpose in what I was doing; that they also saw the urgent need for preventive action with regard to the safety of these vulnerable girls, and if not on legal grounds then at least on some moral ones.

Betty, as it turned out, was all of that and a whole lot more. As I explained my complicated story to her, she appeared to feel everything I had been feeling and to truly understand the extent of the shock, fear, despair, outrage, and sense of injustice that I had been living with throughout this entire ordeal. She was also moved by how much love I had for these two young children, who were not even my own flesh and blood, and to what great lengths I was willing to travel to ensure that they would not become future victims of sexual abuse. Though our call ended that night without any resolution, I felt relieved to have found someone who truly believed in my cause.

Just as important as believing in my cause was the fact that Betty also refused to give up and let it go. In fact, I was pleasantly surprised when I awakened the next day to find a voicemail on my cell phone from her! Speaking in her gentle tone of voice, Betty had left me a carefully worded message in which she disclosed that she had never before called back a crisis caller… never, that is, until now. However, she had done so in my case, because my unique story had stayed in her mind long after we had gotten off the phone.

Along with her acknowledgment, she had taken it upon herself to personally contact a CPS intake worker in the county where Kim and her daughters lived. Betty said she had already spoken with this individual, and thereby cleared the way for me to report my concerns directly to him in a safe and anonymous manner. Regardless of the apparent disinterest and lack of support shown by the local police, Betty assured me that the county's CPS remained concerned for the girls and eager to hear back from me.

This was, of course, fantastic news, as the email message from my police official friend had given me the impression that CPS would only act if first summoned by the cops, but now I felt as though Betty had, through her status as a crisis counselor, captured the interest and support of CPS. From where I was at in this troubling case, I couldn't have been more grateful. Thanks to the guidance from this guardian angel, a new door had suddenly opened and I walked right in.

Chapter Sixteen

Approaching CPS and a Lawyer

The morning of Wednesday, February 6, 2013, was the first bright and beautiful day I had seen in quite a long time. Not due to the outside weather, but because it was the day I would get to take some action for Lisa and Laura. Though I was certainly not a morning person, I made sure to be up and alert on time for the process that lay ahead.

Shortly after 8 a.m. I placed a call to CPS in the county where Kim and her daughters resided. The intake officer had been expecting to hear from me, and upon connecting, we quickly got down to business. I gave this gentleman all the information he requested over the following half-hour. This consisted of providing him with Kim and her daughters' names, as well as the ages of the two girls. I also gave him Kim's home address, and all the information that I had acquired on Charlie Jones and his criminal history.

Along with explaining the entire situation in detail, including of course what just took place over the weekend, I especially tried to impress upon the intake officer the fact that Kim had a significant disability and was a vulnerable adult. I hoped that placing focus on how she was legally blind and unable to drive would help CPS understand how a single mom in such circumstances could become easy prey to a predatory offender. If CPS could gain an appreciation of Kim's unique difficulties, along with full knowledge of Charlie's documented sexual deviancy toward young girls, perhaps they would be more likely to intervene to ensure the well-being of her children.

Though the intake officer was quite polite and kind in demeanor, he made it clear that he was not legally allowed to update me on the status of my report in the future. "Yes, you may call again at any time if you have new information," he told me. "However, I most likely will not be able to tell you anything from our end in regard to this matter."

Though I felt some satisfaction in being able to call CPS, I still felt as though there was more that I could be doing to help Lisa and Laura. With the situation heavily on my mind, I began to wonder if more could be done through the legal system to intervene. After talking with one of my friends who is an experienced attorney, she referred me to an excellent lawyer who specializes in family law matters.

On Thursday, February 7, I met with the family law attorney that my friend had recommended. Upon presenting her with all the information, she explained to me that the only person in the girls' lives with any legal power whatsoever was their biological father. "If you, sir were the biological father of these two young girls, you would have a strong case today for getting full custody of them from their mother, Kim, given the awful circumstances," she told me. She also surprised me by informing me that even Kim's parents, the girls' maternal grandparents who were very involved in their lives, had no legal rights or powers in this situation. Therefore, in order to put a stop to her allowing Charlie to spend overnights, I realized I would need to work toward getting the girls' father more involved.

I also got confirmation during this lawyer meeting that Charlie had indeed violated his court-imposed probation on two separate occasions over the years, in May 2007 and February 2008. This information was revealed when the lawyer I consulted used a state court website to look up more detailed information about Charlie's legal history and records. Apparently, the legal system had gone easy on Charlie for the May 2007 violation, but had not been so forgiving when he did it again in February 2008. Though it did not say what he had specifically done on these two occasions to violate the terms and conditions of his probation, although I suspected it might have involved having illegal contact with female minors, the February 2008 violation was the one that resulted in him being sent to state prison for hard time in March 2008. This information, along with his current behavior of spending overnights, served to reinforce my long held belief that Charlie was likely not rehabilitated and a continued threat to young girls.

Fortunately, exciting news of Dave's attempts at involvement would soon be coming my way. On the afternoon of Monday, February 11, my parents' wedding anniversary; I received a wonderful, surprising voicemail message from my good friend Joan. She told me that Dave and his mother Kathy had met earlier this morning with CPS officials in the city, and had reported their concerns about the well-being of Lisa and Laura. I felt utterly relieved and delighted upon receiving this great information.

I then spoke on the phone with Joan shortly after getting her message, and was thrilled to learn that she was back on board with being involved in this matter. "I got a call from Dave's mother Kathy today, Sumi, and she told me that she and Dave had approached CPS… and that CPS was apparently waiting to hear from them!" She was surprised that CPS already knew about the matter, as I hadn't told her that I had contacted them myself on February 6. She then informed me that Kathy had instructed her to call the police department's non-emergency number and make a CPS report each time, when and if, Joan was to see Charlie come to Kim's home while the girls were present. Though Joan had backed off after being threatened by the local police, she was now willing to become involved again due to the endorsement from CPS.

Given these reported, proposed actions by CPS as stated to Joan by Kathy, I again felt deeply confused over whether or not Charlie was legally allowed to be around the girls. So, later that day, I called CPS and spoke again with the same intake officer whom I had talked with the week before. Though he couldn't give me much information on what was now occurring, I did manage to wrestle two important facts out of him. First, he finally explained to me what had apparently caused the big discrepancy in how law enforcement and CPS were addressing the issue of Charlie being near female minors. "Well, I am probably telling you too much already, but the reason why the police didn't arrest him is because Charlie's PO is okay with him spending overnights near Kim's daughters," is what he shockingly told me.

I was flabbergasted at receiving this disturbing information! After all, a sex offender's probation officer is the one person who is supposed to enforce his restrictions and do everything to ensure that he stays far away from trouble, and now I'm hearing that the PO is reportedly the one who is allowing the overnight contact with minors? It was yet another ugly twist in this complicated matter. Along with this revealing information, the intake officer also gave me the name and contact info of the CPS staff member who was currently handling the investigation.

As it turned out, Dave and Kathy's visit to CPS appeared to have more of an immediate impact on Kim than when I had contacted CPS the prior week, most likely because Dave and Kathy were the girls' immediate biological family. On the day after their visit to CPS, Tuesday, February 12, I suddenly received a text message from Kim indicating that she was now aware of CPS's involvement.

> "I just wanted you to know that I have ended my relationship with Charlie. Too stressful dating a registered sex offender. I already feel much relieved at having made this decision. I just couldn't handle social services stepping into the situation."

Interestingly, Joan soon informed me that she had also received a similar text message on this same day from Kim. Joan's text message from Kim read as follows:

"I just want you to know that I am very sorry for everything that has recently happened. I have ended my relationship with Charlie. I have lost the contact information I once had for Dave's brother, but please go ahead and tell him for me that Charlie and I have stopped seeing one another."

Naturally, both Joan and I were quite suspicious of Kim's intentions in sending us these strikingly similar text messages. Given all she had done in order to remain with Charlie, in spite of knowing his record and the significant risk to her daughters, we had a difficult time now trusting her word that she had broken things off. Sure enough, a quick check of Charlie's Facebook page would confirm our joint suspicions. Within a day or two, I observed a Facebook message that a supposedly despondent Charlie had posted on Tuesday, February 12, which displayed his alleged self-pity and pathetically stated, "I am done trying to be happy. I am done dating."

Following this post were a few sympathetic comments made by those close to Charlie, including one by his own mother. Then the following morning, Wednesday, February 13, a day after Kim had sent Joan and me the texts claiming they had broken up, there was a new posting from Kim to Charlie on his Facebook page at 11:12 a.m., which now stated, "I love you. You're still mine." Obviously, Joan and I took this disturbing comment, along with the fact that she and Charlie were still connected on Facebook, as evidence that their relationship had not truly come to an end. Instead, it appeared as though Kim had simply tried to manipulate us.

So later I contacted the CPS officer who was currently handling the investigation. Along with introducing myself and explaining my role in this matter, I informed the officer of my concerns regarding Charlie's PO as well as about Kim's Facebook comment indicating that she was still involved with Charlie. The investigator gave me her cell phone number and told me to call her anytime if I ever have information that Charlie is coming near Kim's daughters. On the negative side, she claimed that it is not the duty of CPS to determine whether Charlie's PO is within his legal rights to allow the predatory offender to spend overnights near Lisa and Laura. The CPS officer also put me off by saying that this case was a lower priority in the eyes of CPS. "Basically, we have to wait until something actually happens before we can take further action," she explained to me. Needless to say, I was quite let down and disappointed to hear this. After all, my whole goal was to have intervention BEFORE anything happened to Lisa and Laura!

Given my recent discoveries from talking with CPS and the lawyer, I felt that there was more that I still needed to do for the girls. I would need to encourage their father Dave to take a more active approach, and to somehow get to the bottom of what was up with Charlie's PO.

Chapter Seventeen

Appeal to Relatives and Those in Higher Power (Part One)

In spite of some recent progress with CPS, the whole Charlie ordeal was beginning to take its toll on me. Right along with all the frustrations and setbacks, was the fact that I was missing Lisa and Laura. My efforts to protect them and keep them safe had gotten them ripped right out of my life. At times, I couldn't help but stop and feel a bit sorry for myself. What had I possibly done wrong to deserve this outcome? I couldn't help but imagine how many mothers of molested kids would have killed to have a friend like me to warn them about a guy like Charlie before their precious children ever came in harm's way. Yet the mother in this particular case had taken a much different stance. The result was that her girls were not safe and I had managed to lose them as well.

By Monday, February 18, I reached a really low point. Joan was trying again to get in touch with Dave's family and was not having any luck. Specifically, she had sent a long Facebook message to Dave's brother Nathan, in which she had given him my cell number and instructed him to give me a call. When he had not called me by day's end, I truly hit rock bottom.

Needless to say, I did not sleep well that night. The next morning, shortly after 8 a.m., I called the CPS officer who was investigating Charlie's case. Upon connecting with her, I asked her if CPS could interview the girls about whether he had spent overnights there. The lady merely responded by saying she could not tell me whether they would do so or not. I also asked her if CPS can at least educate the girls on what to do if they are abused, and again she said she couldn't give me any information about it. Having exhausted these options, I then emailed the CPS officer an eight-page statement I had typed, which summarized all of my concerns in the Charlie matter. It made me feel a bit better to ensure that CPS knew everything.

Later, on Tuesday, February 19, at about 4:30 p.m., I finally received the long-awaited phone call from Dave's brother Nathan. Unfortunately, it did not go as well as I had hoped. Though Nathan was polite and friendly, I soon found that he appeared more interested in leaving the entire matter to CPS. This was a setback, as I was hoping to persuade him to get Dave to take stronger actions for Lisa and Laura. Furthermore, Nathan also disclosed to me that he had not even read any of the paperwork that Joan had left for him concerning Charlie's criminal history. I felt this was a devastating blow, as those papers contained all the info on what a great threat Charlie posed to the girls. These girls were Nathan's nieces, his very own flesh and blood, and I couldn't understand why he didn't seem more enthused to step up and take charge. It was a helpless feeling knowing that he had chosen not to read them at all, as I knew that the girls' father was unable to read anything on his own.

Although frustrated and defeated yet again, I tried to dust myself off and move on. I spent the next two days making phone calls and searching online to find the immediate boss of Charlie's PO. Upon locating this individual on Thursday, February 21, I emailed her a long letter explaining my concerns about the PO allowing Charlie to spend overnights near Lisa and Laura. Naturally, I was greatly disturbed at the thought that this PO might indeed be favoring Charlie in an unprofessional manner. Along with what I had heard about him from CPS, I was concerned over how Kim had previously disclosed to me that the PO supposedly took Charlie's side in all matters. I was also more suspicious about this because I had since learned through Joan's investigating on Facebook that Charlie's mother used to work for our state's judicial system. Could Charlie's mom somehow be connected with this probation officer through a prior working relationship?

Regardless, in addressing the boss of Charlie's PO, I had to pick and choose my words carefully, as I wanted to communicate my concerns clearly without getting anyone overly agitated. Here is the letter I sent to the boss of Charlie's PO, with some changes made in regards to the actual names of the people involved:

Dear (Name given),

I am approaching you here with a good faith concern regarding an offender, Charles Michael Jones (DOB given), currently being supervised by one of your probation officers, (Name given). I am not sending this email to make a complaint or to cause any trouble, but rather merely to seek some better clarification and understanding on some clarity of guidelines that the probation officers are supposed to follow when enforcing restrictions upon the offenders they supervise. I would earnestly request that my name and identity please remain confidential from the probation officer and from the offender Charles Michael Jones as I simply mean to explore my concern further with you.

Charles Michael Jones is a convicted child molester and is believed to be a predatory offender (as per publicly available records). As per these available public records, there are significant restrictions currently in place with regards to Mr. Jones' ability to come into contact with female minors. Over the past month, Mr. Jones has begun to date a friend of mine who is a single mother with two young

95

daughters, ages 13 and 10, and who is living in (County given). Although I did a background check on Mr. Jones and quickly made my friend aware of his noted history of felony criminal sexual conduct with the young female child of a previous woman he was partnered with, my friend has still opted to continue to date Mr. Jones regardless of my warning.

While dating Mr. Jones is my friend's personal choice to make for herself as an adult, I have grown more concerned as she has also chosen to allow Mr. Jones near her minor daughters on multiple recent occasions. In fact, I personally witnessed Mr. Jones being at my friend's residence and interacting with her daughters on Sunday, January 20, 2013. Within an hour or so of Mr. Jones' arrival at my friend's house on that evening, local law enforcement arrived at the residence and spent an hour speaking with my friend and with Mr. Jones about the restrictions around his contact with female minors.

On that particular evening, I personally witnessed local law enforcement inform my friend that Mr. Jones is NOT permitted to spend an overnight at my friend's home if her young daughters are also present underneath the same roof. The police also stated that Mr. Jones cannot be alone with my friend's daughters at all, so that if my friend were to use the restroom, Mr. Jones would have to step outside the residence and only return inside once my friend was done and out of the restroom.

Based upon this understanding, I became gravely concerned when I was contacted by a reliable eyewitness in my friend's neighborhood, who informed me that she personally observed that Mr. Jones did indeed spend at least one, if not two overnights at my friend's residence and with her minor daughters also present, over the weekend of Friday, February 1 – Sunday, February 3, 2013. I also have an email sent to me in my inbox by my friend on the early morning of Sunday, February 3, in which she states in writing that Mr. Jones was indeed at the residence late Saturday night and playing a board game with my friend and her daughters. As it turned out, local police were called to my friend's home again late on Saturday, February 2 in relation to this concern, but apparently this time they allowed Mr. Jones to remain at the residence with the minor children and in turn strongly advised the reliable eyewitness in my friend's neighborhood to NEVER call them about this concern!

Since this occurred, the grave concern for the well-being of my friend's minor children around this predatory offender has been reported to CPS by myself, as well as by the biological father of my friend's two daughters. When speaking personally with a CPS intake worker, I expressed my genuine confusion over the discrepancy in how local law enforcement handled these issues, being that their approach varied greatly from when they were called to my friend's home on January 20, 2013, in comparison to when they were called out again on February 02, 2013. In response to my inquiry about this, the intake worker replied by saying that Mr.

Jones was apparently permitted to spend an overnight at my friend's residence with her daughters present, reportedly because "his probation officer did not have a problem with it."

I am writing to you to seek better clarification on whether the probation officer does in fact have the discretion to allow this offender to spend overnights with minor females present in a home. If it is well within the probation officer's rights to allow it, then of course there are no confusions or issues. However, if it remains true that Mr. Jones is NOT permitted to spend an overnight around minor female children, as was explained by police in my presence on January 20, 2013, then I remain gravely concerned about the fact that the offender did spend time overnight over the weekend of February 1 – February 3. I am also more concerned, because I am aware from viewing public records that Mr. Jones has apparently violated his probation twice before, in May 2007 and February 2008, which I believe resulted in him being sent to state prison for a period of time and for which he is now out on supervised release.

I would really appreciate your thoughts and insights into this matter. If it is necessary to be disclosed, I can provide the identity and contact information of the reliable eyewitness in the neighborhood who personally observed that Mr. Jones spent at least one overnight at my friend's residence with her minor daughters also present over the weekend of February 1 – February 3. I can also forward you the email from my friend, which further places Mr.

Jones there with both minor females present late at night on Saturday, February 2, 2013.

I greatly appreciate your willingness to look into this matter, and I anticipate to hear back from you at your earliest convenience. Once again, my intent here is not to make a complaint or cause any trouble, my intent is simply to understand a possible inconsistency.

Sincerely,

Sumi

Tragically, I soon learned that this lady was on vacation and would be out of the office for another full week, until Thursday, February 28. It seemed as though this case continued to kick me square in the teeth.

Fortunately, one positive thing was about to occur. Over the weekend I agreed to watch Mark and Mike as their parents were flying out of state, and while hanging out with them on Sunday, February 24, I suddenly received a text message from none other than little Laura! It was exactly four weeks to the day since I'd heard from her last, and that had been the angry text where she blamed me for "ruining" things with her mother and Charlie, but this time, I was relieved to see that it appeared Laura had forgotten all about that. She initiated contact by saying "hi" and then it snowballed from there, with us texting back and forth making small talk, asking one another how we had been. Laura also happened to mention that she and Lisa were currently at their dad's this weekend, and that Lisa was apparently bothering her. It touched me so deeply to have heard from Laura and to know that our love and great times had not been forgotten.

The texting with Laura and time with the boys was a true blessing, especially in light of the ongoing hassles that lay ahead. The very next day, on Monday, February 25, Joan notified me of a new posting on Charlie's Facebook page, which clearly demonstrated that, he and Kim were moving forward in their romantic relationship. This of course concerned me greatly for the well-being of Lisa and Laura, both of whom would be with their mother that upcoming weekend. Alarmed I then copied the posting, which included a joyful picture of Kim and Charlie close together and laughing, and emailed it to the CPS investigator who was working the case. I also voiced to her my concerns about the girls' safety for the upcoming weekend.

As was quickly becoming a pattern, I did not hear back at all from the CPS investigator upon sending her this information, but instead of leaving it at that, I urged Joan to contact Dave's mother and let her know about this latest development. I wanted to do everything humanly possible to prevent the girls from enduring another weekend with that convicted child molester around them, and when Joan for some reason was having difficulties in calling Kathy, I looked up her number on my own and called her myself.

On the evening of Tuesday, February 26, I spoke on the phone for forty-five minutes with Kathy. Our long conversation was extremely positive, and she came across as a rather sweet and caring grandmother. She also seemed to care a lot for her son, Dave, and openly shared with me about his learning disability and other related issues.

Along with introducing myself and my role in this matter to Kathy, I updated her about how Kim had Charlie over during the weekend of February 1 – 3, while the girls were near him in the house. I also told her about the recently observed interaction on Facebook between Kim and Charlie, which demonstrated that their relationship was escalating. I then also told her all about the New Year's Eve incident at Kim's house with that guy Rick, and how that specific event had prompted me to do the revealing background check two weeks later on Charlie. Though Kathy had

100

not known about the Rick incident, she had indeed read all the paperwork on Charlie's criminal history that Joan had left with her other son Nathan. Even so, I made sure to fill her in on everything I knew about the convicted child molester who appeared to be honing in on her young granddaughters.

After informing Kathy about my concerns for Lisa and Laura that upcoming weekend, she informed me that she would be contacting the CPS investigator on the following day to pursue getting an Order of Protection. This legal option, Kathy explained to me, would be an attempt by her and Dave to get the girls out of Kim's home and custody. "Kim and Charlie can fondle each other all they want," Kathy told me, "but I think we outta focus on getting those girls out of there if we can."

My conversation with Kathy seemed to be my very first stroke of good luck. Now, hopefully, the girls would be safe by the time the weekend arrived.

Chapter Eighteen

Appeal to Relatives and Those in Higher Power (Part Two)

After having waited for what felt like an eternity, Thursday, February 28, had finally rolled around. This was the day of course, that the boss of Charlie's PO would be back in her office and able to read my long email. Sure enough, this lady called and left me a voicemail early in the morning when I was still asleep. Unfortunately, her somewhat confusing message seemed to indicate that she had missed the whole point of my email.

In her voicemail message, this lady informed me that the DOC supposedly informs family members, the police, and CPS if someone is dating a registered sex offender. Perhaps she was stating what was done in other cases or in general, because that was certainly **not** what had occurred in this situation. On the contrary, it was me who had done the background check and informed my friend Kim, the police in several counties, CPS and eventually Dave's side of the family. I was surprised and confused at receiving her general message, which did nothing to address the specific situation with Charlie. Even though I happened to be leaving on this day for an out-of-state business trip, I still called this lady from the airport and was lucky enough to connect.

However, it seemed as though that is where my good fortune would end. Upon speaking with this woman, I first clarified who she was and that she had actually read my lengthy email letter, but once I began attempting to discuss the PO issue, she cut me off by saying that she could not give me any specifics on Charlie's case. The only thing she did say was to inform me that none of the recent events I had relayed to her in my email, such as Charlie spending overnights near Lisa and Laura, apparently constituted a violation of Charlie's current probation conditions.

When I pressed her further about how his current records state that he is **not** allowed contact with females under eighteen, she replied by saying that an offender's stated restrictions can change over time, if he completes treatment and behaves in a positive manner. The lady also seemed puzzled as to why I was concerned about Charlie dating Kim, given that Kim wanted to continue to see him. It certainly seemed to me as though this lady was missing the point.

Though the conversation was not going as I had hoped, I quickly found an opening with which to regain her concern and interest. Specifically, I took issue with her statement that an offender's restrictions can change if he completes treatment and behaves well. I told her about how Charlie had convinced my disabled, single-mother friend Kim into wrongly believing that he was innocent, and that the little girl he was convicted of molesting was nothing but a liar.

At last, this lady now appeared to understand why I was so concerned. She now seemed shocked and upset that Charlie had lied about his guilt in discussions with Kim, and also deeply concerned to learn that Kim was a more vulnerable adult with some form of disability. Observing the positive change in her demeanor, I continued to drive home my main point to this lady. I made the argument that since sex offender treatment is all about **admitting** one's guilt and accepting full responsibility, how can anyone say that Charlie has successfully completed treatment and is deserving of less restrictions when according to Kim he was still proclaiming his innocence? Our conversation ended with this lady acknowledging my concerns and saying that she would "look into this matter further." However, as it turned out, I would not hear back from the woman again.

Not yet knowing this, I still sent her a follow-up email on the early morning of Friday, March 1, right from my hotel room during my business trip. In this second lengthy email, I further explained Kim's disability in greater detail, along with all the other troubling aspects of this Charlie ordeal. I tried my best to get this lady to feel some compassion and understand how particularly vulnerable Lisa and Laura were in this situation, especially given the fact that both of their parents have significant disabilities. Though I did place particular focus on this aspect, it is important to note that families without disability related issues are also vulnerable to skilled predators, of which there are many out there.

Along with my effort in contacting the boss of Charlie's PO, I had long been considering the idea of reaching out to the trial judge who had convicted and sentenced Charlie for his crime back in 2004. I had thought about informing the judge, as he was the one who had originally decided that Charlie was not allowed contact with girls under the age of eighteen. As it turned out, one of my lawyer friends had heard of this judge and was willing to check with her colleagues to see if she could set up a meeting between the judge and me, but by day's end I had not yet heard back from her. I was also unable to get hold of Joan by phone or Facebook on that evening, and was unable to know if Charlie was over again at Kim's house.

On Saturday, March 2, I returned home during the afternoon from my business trip and was finally able to get ahold of Joan. Unfortunately, all she could tell me was that she did not know where Kim and the girls were this weekend. Concerned for them once again, I decided to call Kathy and check with her if she had indeed contacted CPS in pursuit of the Order of Protection that we had spoken about Tuesday night.

Tragically, upon connecting with Kathy I could not have been more let down and disappointed. Incredibly, Kathy informed me that she had been too busy that week with friends being in town to get around to pursuing the Order of Protection. I simply could not fathom how the girls' very own grandmother did not appear to be taking this matter seriously enough. I mean, here I was, not even a blood relative to Lisa and Laura, and I am unable to relax not knowing if Charlie was around them again that weekend, and Kathy, the only person who can help Dave assert his parental rights, was too busy hanging out with her pals? *Your granddaughters are your first priority lady*, I felt like screaming at her!

On the positive side, Kathy did again say that she was planning to discuss the issue with Dave the following day, and that they were still planning to take some form of action. I remained concerned, however, especially given the fact that Joan and her family would be leaving for a ten-day vacation on Thursday, March 7. Once they left town, there would be nobody across the street to observe and alert CPS should Charlie attempt to come near Kim and the girls. I made sure to pass this concern along to the CPS investigator, who once again declined to even acknowledge my existence.

Over the next week, I heard back from my lawyer friend who informed me that she was unable to set up a meeting between myself and the judge in Charlie's case. Regardless, I went ahead with putting together a long letter for the judge, and my lawyer friend agreed to review it before I mailed it to him. At least I could relax about the girls' safety over the following weekend, as they would be with their father from Friday, March 8 to Sunday, March 10. In fact, on Sunday and Monday, I would have the unexpected pleasure of receiving text messages again from little Laura. Although I, of course, texted back to her, I made sure to document for myself that Laura had reached out to me first on these days, just in case Kim would later find out and attempt to fault me as the one initiating contact with her children.

On Tuesday, March 12, I received my first text messages and form of contact from Lisa since I had seen her last on January 21. Laura texted me on this day as well. As it turned out, the girls were off school for spring break that week, and they contacted me while their mother was at work. Lisa then even called me from her **iPad**, and we were able to chat for a while. During our texts and conversation, Lisa sent me pictures of her bunny and of her in new glasses that she had recently gotten. She also told me that she had been named Student of the Month for March, and I told her how proud I was of her. It was such a treat to communicate with the girls again, and I so wished that I could see them just as I had in the past.

Along with hearing from the girls on March 12, I also received the corrections my lawyer friend had made to my letter for Charlie's judge on this same day. My friend had offered to review the document to ensure that my message would be as effective as possible. She also wanted to make sure that I didn't say anything in my letter that could be used against me or could constitute defamation of character toward anyone. Defamation of character refers to saying something about someone that is not based on fact for which you can later get sued in a court of law. Here is the finalized version of the letter I would soon be mailing to the judge who presided over Charlie's case, with some changes to the actual names of people involved:

Dear Honorable Judge (Name Given),

Good day, Your Honor. I am writing you about my grave concern for the welfare of two minor children who I believe are vulnerable and may become victims to a man that was convicted of child molestation in your Court in approximately May 2004. I do not know how else to try and protect these young girls since I am not a family member, but merely a family friend who is aware of the menacing situation.

It is my understanding that Defendant Charles Michael Jones (DOB Given) was found guilty of committing sexual abuse of a female minor back in

May 2004. It is my understanding that you sentenced him in August 2004, regarding two counts of second-degree criminal sexual conduct. Again, based on my understanding of his criminal history, Mr. Jones violated your court imposed probation at least twice over the following years (in May 2007 and February 2008), and as a result was sent to state prison in March 2008 to serve time. Records show that he was released from incarceration in February 2009. Mr. Jones is currently out of prison on supervised release, which does not expire until February 2014.

I am greatly concerned because as of mid-January, a very close friend of mine began dating Mr. Jones. This friend is a vulnerable adult; a disabled, legally-blind, divorced, single mother with two young daughters, ages 13 and 10. She is unable to operate a motor vehicle, and is fully dependent upon others for all of her and her children's transportation needs. I had dated this woman briefly in the summer of 2011, but we decided over time to keep it at friendship. As a result of that relationship, I became a very close father figure and regular caretaker of her two young daughters.

My friend, Kim, and her two minor daughters reside in (County Name Given). I had suspicions regarding Mr. Jones when I learned he was dating my friend. I did a background check on Mr. Jones when I first learned from Facebook that my friend had now suddenly met and begun dating Mr. Jones in mid-January. I did this background check simply to ensure the future safety of my friend's two daughters, whose biological father is also disabled and whom I've grown to love and care for as if they were my own.

When I discovered Mr. Jones's disturbing history of second-degree criminal sexual conduct for molesting the eleven-year-old daughter of the woman he was married to in December 2002, I promptly shared this information with my friend, fully intending to warn and protect them on Saturday, January 19, 2013. However, shockingly my friend then immediately heard Mr. Jones's version of events and has very poorly chosen to believe him and continue to date Mr. Jones. In fact, since the following day, Sunday, January 20, 2013, my friend has allowed Mr. Jones to be around her young daughters on multiple occasions.

As a result of the continued contact that I am aware of regarding Mr. Jones and the two minor girls, both a neighbor and I have contacted the local police and advised them of the situation. I personally witnessed the local police tell my friend at her residence on Sunday, January 20, 2013, that Mr. Jones is NOT permitted to spend an overnight at my friend's home if her young daughters are also present underneath the same roof. The police also stated at that time that Mr. Jones cannot be alone with the daughters at all, so that if my friend were to use the restroom, Mr. Jones would have to step outside the residence and only return inside once my friend was done and out of the restroom.

Based upon this understanding, Your Honor, I became gravely concerned when I was contacted by a reliable eyewitness in my friend's neighborhood, who informed me that she personally observed that Mr. Jones did indeed spend at least one, if not two overnights at my friend's residence, and with her minor daughters also present, over the weekend of Friday, February 1 – Sunday, February 3, 2013. I also have an email sent to me by my friend on the early morning of Sunday, February 3, in which she stated in writing that Mr. Jones was indeed at her residence late Saturday night and playing a board game with my friend and her daughters. See attached email. As it turned out, local police were called to my friend's home again late on Saturday, February 2 in relation to this concern, but apparently this time they allowed Mr. Jones to remain at the residence with the minor children, and in turn, angrily ordered the reliable eyewitness in my friend's neighborhood to NEVER call them about this concern!

Since this shocking, highly unfortunate turn of events, the grave concern for the well-being of my friend's minor children around this predatory offender has been reported to CPS by myself as well as by the biological father of my friend's two daughters, along with his mother who looks after him. When speaking personally with a CPS intake worker, I expressed my genuine confusion over the discrepancy in how local law enforcement handled these issues, being that their approach varied greatly from when they were called to my friend's home on January 20, 2013, in comparison to when they were called out again on February 02, 2013. In response to my inquiry about this, the intake worker replied by saying that Mr. Jones was apparently permitted to spend an overnight at my friend's residence with her minor daughters present, reportedly because "his probation officer did not have a problem with it."

I have since then, Your Honor, taken it upon myself to personally speak with (Name Given), who is the district supervisor of the state department of corrections and who is also the immediate boss of Mr. Jones's probation officer, (Name Given). The lady said she was unable to give me any specifics about Mr. Jones's case, other than to comment that she apparently did not believe that any violations had occurred as of yet.

The lady also explained to me, without going into specifics about Mr. Jones that offenders in general can earn more privileges over time than what is originally stated on their records if they have completed treatment and/or properly followed other conditions of their probation.

However, this lady seemed surprised and taken aback when I then informed her that my single mother friend has a significant disability (a rare one that caused her legal blindness). I also revealed to the lady that my friend has stated to me that Mr. Jones has explained to her that he was supposedly innocent of the molestation charges for which he was convicted by you, Your Honor, and for which the verdicts were also later upheld by an appeals court. The lady seemed concerned about this information, replying that she will "look into this," though I have not yet heard back from her in close to two weeks.

This leaves me with a tremendous sense of concern and injustice, Your Honor, knowing how Mr. Jones has duped my single mom friend into wrongfully believing in his innocence and wrongfully believing that he was railroaded. This makes me seriously question whether Mr. Jones is rehabilitated and should really be permitted to be around the girls in any capacity.

Based on my conversations with my friend, I was also shocked and dismayed to learn that Mr. Jones has referred to his prior young victim as "a liar who kept changing her story" and the victim's mother as "an unreliable drunken woman." This conduct by Mr. Jones, as reported to me by my friend in a face-to-face conversation on Monday, January 21, 2013, evening, is certainly not consistent with the profile of an individual who has successfully completed sex offender treatment and is no longer a risk to the community. That is exactly what my friend had told me Mr. Jones had said to her about his conviction at your hands, Your Honor. I readily attest to that right here in this written statement.

So in summary, Your Honor, I am writing this long letter to see if there is anything that you can do now, within your powers, to possibly intervene in this complicated matter. I have read the newspaper article about your sentencing of Mr. Jones in August 2004, Your Honor, and I simply cannot imagine that spending overnights near female minors is what you had in mind for Mr. Jones when you gave him 25 years of strict probation – specifying NO CONTACT WITH GIRLS YOUNGER THAN 18 WITH THE EXCEPTION OF HIS DAUGHTER. At that sentencing, I read that Mr. Jones told you he was sorry for what happened and said he was afraid of what his life would become. He then asked you for a chance to prove himself.

Even giving Mr. Jones the benefit of the doubt, being allowed around female minors, especially for overnights has got to be subjecting this sex offender to undue amounts of temptation. However more likely, it seems like the behavior of a calculating predatory offender waiting to make his next move on these girls.

Please consider intervening in this matter, Your Honor, to ensure that the strict conditions of the probation that you imposed upon Mr. Jones are being followed and applied in an appropriate manner today by the parties in charge; and in a manner that supports the personal safety interests of any children who may inevitably cross paths with Mr. Jones, and not by their own choosing!

I greatly thank you, Your Honor, for your time and effort spent in reading my long letter. In all honesty, you are my very last hope for protecting these two vulnerable children who are already disadvantaged in their lives and whom I love as if they were my own. I can be reached by cell phone at (763) 300-

8328, by email at sumis@earthlink.net, and of course by my home address. I know you must be very busy, Your Honor, and I appreciate any help you are possibly able to lend to this troubling situation.

Most Sincerely,

Sumi Mukherjee

Interestingly, my lawyer friend was unable to give me a prediction of how the judge might react to my letter, and/or whether he might choose to take some form of action. "This is not a common occurrence Sumi, so there aren't other similar cases that I can refer to in order to make a prediction," my friend explained to me. "I feel that as a judge he would be compelled to do something, but I really can't make a guess as to what he might choose to do."

The next morning, on Wednesday, March 13, I mailed the finalized letter to the judge by express mail service at 10 a.m. meaning it was guaranteed to arrive to the judge by 12 p.m. on Thursday, March 14. I also texted back and forth with Laura in the evening, playfully discussing who was tougher and smarter between the two of us and making small talk. On Thursday, shortly after 9 a.m., I called the courthouse and confirmed that the judge was indeed there that morning. I found out later that afternoon that my letter had been delivered there at 8:22 a.m., even before I made the phone call. Along with texting a bit with Laura, I texted a lot that evening with Lisa. The older sister had contacted me to chat in general, and to tell me about a high school boy who she now claimed to be dating! Though I wasn't sure if I believed her story, I told Lisa that I was proud of her in general and that I love her and miss her a lot.

Although I had taken an important step by contacting the judge, I still remained concerned about the upcoming weekend. With Joan and her family far away out of town, I began to worry if

Kim might try to invite Charlie over again.

Chapter Nineteen

A New Dangerous Close Encounter

Right from the very start, the entire situation with Charlie had been all about trusting my gut instinct and from the moment Joan had told me that she and her family would be out of town for ten days in March, my gut instinct had told me that there would be trouble.

Fortunately, Joan had arranged for her close friend Michelle to watch her elderly mother at Joan's house while she and the rest of her family were away. Though I had tried to resist the urge to check in with Michelle Friday night, I broke down and decided to text her shortly before 8 a.m. on the morning of Saturday, March 16. Following a little small talk with Michelle, I finally sent her a text directly concerning the Charlie issue at 7:54 a.m. "Have you noticed that guy visiting at all across the street?" I attempted to ask in a nonchalant manner.

Of course, Michelle knew exactly whom I was referring to, as she had been there with Joan on the disastrous night of Saturday, February 2 when the local police had chewed Joan out for trespassing on Kim's property. In a strange and contradictory answer, Michelle replied back by saying, "No, haven't noticed but really not watching. I saw a car pull in the garage last night." Alarmed at this info, I immediately texted Michelle again and asked her to confirm the color of the car she had observed pulling into Kim's garage last night. When she declined to reply to me, I decided to forego the texting and instead just gave her a call.

Sure enough, upon connecting by phone with her, she went on to confirm my long-held suspicions that Charlie was indeed over at Kim's. As we spoke on the phone Saturday morning, Michelle told me she observed Charlie's car pulling into Kim's garage the previous night between 9 and 10 p.m. Seeking proof that the vehicle was still currently in the garage, I asked Michelle if she would please walk into Kim's backyard and take a peek in the back window of her garage. "Ok, I'll do it, but just don't tell anyone Sumi, cause I don't wanna get in trouble for trespassing like Joan did!" she said. After I promised her that I wouldn't say anything, Michelle got off the phone and walked into Kim's backyard. Moments later, she called me back and confirmed that Charlie's car was indeed still inside her garage. This meant that convicted child molester Charlie Jones had arrived at Kim's last night, and had spent the overnight again at her house with Lisa and Laura inside.

With that piece of information, I suddenly found myself thrust back into the same living hell I had experienced over the dreadful weekend of February 2. All of a sudden, my heart was pounding in my chest as a sense of terror came upon me. Is he going to molest the girls this time around? Did he already do it last night? Is he doing it to them right at this very moment? Those were the only thoughts that flowed through my tortured mind. Overwhelmed as I felt, I knew I had to take immediate action.

After getting off the phone with Michelle, I decided to follow the procedure that Dave's mother had laid out for Joan right after Dave and Kathy's visit last month with CPS. Back then, Kathy had instructed Joan to call the police department's non-emergency number and leave a report for CPS, when and if Joan were to ever observe Charlie coming near Lisa and Laura. With Joan out of town and out of the country, I knew I needed to take on this responsibility myself.

In spite of my fearing the repercussions of contacting the police department in Kim's county, I called their non-emergency number and spoke with the operator. I explained the circumstances to this lady as relayed to me by eyewitness Michelle, except for leaving out the fact that she had trespassed onto Kim's property. The lady told me she would have an officer call me soon regarding my concerns. However, I was never contacted by anyone from the police department.

Regardless of not receiving the promised call from an officer, I also left a voicemail message and email with the CPS investigator who was assigned to Charlie's case. As usual, I did not hear back from her either. Below is the email I sent that Saturday morning to the CPS investigator, with some changes made to ensure the privacy of the actual parties involved:

From: Sumi Mukherjee<sumis@earthlink.net>

To: CPS Investigator

Subject: Report of Charlie Jones overnight with minor girls

Date: Mar 16, 2013 8:46 AM

Dear Investigator,

I spoke to a woman this morning between 8 a.m. - 8:30 a.m., she is the friend who is watching Kim's neighbor Joan's house while Joan is on vacation out of the country. The woman told me she saw a car quickly pull into Kim's garage last night, Friday, March 15th, between 9-10 p.m. The woman says the car is (color given) and is still in Kim's garage right now, as of 8:36 a.m. Saturday morning, March 16th. Charlie Jones drives a (car type described) with (license plate number given).

Based on this information, I have reason to strongly believe that convicted child molester Charlie Jones spent the overnight at Kim's home, and is still there right now. I'm concerned and reporting this as instructed, because Kim's two minor daughters are in her care for this entire weekend, and are most likely present in the house with Charlie right now.

Much like before, all luck in this frustrating matter appeared to be on the side of the predatory offender. Unable to get ahold of the police or CPS, I decided to turn my efforts once again in the direction of Dave's family. After briefly playing phone tag that morning, I had a conversation with Dave's brother Nathan and fully updated him on the risks his nieces were facing that weekend.

Amazingly, in spite of the horror of knowing the girls were currently near Charlie, Nathan had what appeared to be very encouraging news to share with me. He informed me that Dave had recently met with people on Thursday to work toward getting his daughters away from Kim. In fact, he said that Dave was planning to try to get an Order of Protection for the girls as early as Monday, and to also get some kind of order against Kim. Nathan said that Dave had been meeting with people who worked with a local domestic violence center, and that those folks were the ones who were advising Dave in this matter.

Nathan also shared that he felt we must not do anything to tip Kim and Charlie off about this pending legal action, as the people at the domestic violence center had warned Dave that the desperate pair might attempt to kidnap the girls and leave the state if they learned what was coming! Of all the concerns that had gone through my mind, even I had not yet considered the possibility of them kidnapping Lisa and Laura. Horrified as I was at that idea, I felt relieved and excited to know that significant action appeared to be on the way. I was also grateful to have had such a positive interaction with Nathan, who seemed to open up and display the care and concern I'd expected before.

However, no form of action could come quickly enough to tame my concerns about the girls' safety that weekend. Knowing that Charlie was likely still over there, I left another voicemail and email message for the CPS investigator later on Saturday evening. Below is the second email I sent her in the early evening:

From: Sumi Mukherjee <sumis@earthlink.net>

To: CPS Investigator

Subject: Report to Sheriff's Office

Date: Mar 16, 2013 5:50 PM

Hello Investigator. Just sending you a quick note to inform you that I reported my concern from this morning to the local sheriff's office and spoke with a receptionist. That person took my contact info and told me that an officer would be calling me to speak with me about my concern.

However, about eight hours have now passed and no officer has contacted me. I am extremely, extremely concerned knowing that, in all likelihood, Charlie Jones has now been around Kim's daughters since 9-10 p.m. last night, and will quite likely remain there through the weekend. Charlie committed his previous crime overnight, and I cannot emphasize enough how concerned I am for the well-being of those two young girls in his presence.

I tried contacting the police, and essentially got nowhere. I have left you another voicemail relaying this information as well. I pray that something can be done to keep these children safe. I'm trying to follow the proper channels in reporting my concerns and to continue to have faith in the system to protect children.

I really hope you are able to help in some way, shape or form.

Although I still did not hear back from the CPS investigator, I felt good about sending out a second email. I wanted there to be written documentation of my many attempts to alert the proper authorities about my concerns regarding the children. If the girls were to be sexually abused by Charlie that weekend, God forbid, I at least wanted documentation present so that CPS would be aware that they were forewarned.

Saturday continued to remain an extremely stressful day for me, as I was forced to go on not knowing what was happening to Lisa and Laura. However, at 9 p.m., I would receive an update from Michelle. In a phone call, she told me that she had just observed Charlie, Kim, and both girls arriving back to Kim's house in Charlie's car from an apparent outing. Seeing how this eyewitness information positively identified Charlie being near Lisa and Laura, I left yet a third voicemail/email message for the CPS investigator:

From: Sumi Mukherjee <sumis@earthlink.net>

To: CPS Investigator

Subject: Charlie Identified With Girls Tonight

Date: Mar 16, 2013 9:15 PM

Hi Investigator. Just got a call from Michelle who is
watching Joan's house, and Michelle just informed
me that at 8:45 p.m. Michelle saw Charlie Jones,
Kim, and both girls arriving in Charlie's car at
Kim's home and pulling into the garage together.

This positively places Charlie Jones with the female
minors tonight.

Regardless of all my efforts, nothing in the world could
relieve me of my concerns for the girls on that evening. There was
simply no way for me to feel at peace with the thought that they
might be getting molested by Charlie. Yet, once again, I was
powerless to do anything more to protect them. The feelings of
distress were unbearable as I struggled through another tough
night.

By the grace of God, on Sunday, March 17, early afternoon, I
was finally contacted by the CPS investigator, and I was happy to
see that she appeared disturbed over the fact that I had not been
contacted as promised yesterday by the local police. While she had
me on the phone, the investigator asked me once again to confirm
the timing of how long I believe Charlie had been around Lisa and
Laura that weekend, beginning from when he reportedly arrived at
Kim's residence on Friday evening. "Is he still over there right
now, do you know by chance?" the investigator asked me. Though
I told her I was unsure, I said I would call Michelle and try to find
out if Charlie was there.

Upon getting ahold of Michelle, she said she would try and
call Kim to get some info out of her about Charlie's current
whereabouts, without tipping Kim off that CPS had been inquiring.
I then gave Michelle Kim's cell phone number and waited

anxiously. Several minutes later I heard back from Michelle. "Sorry it took me so long, but Kim just talked my ear off," she explained to me.

Incredibly, she then went on to tell me that Kim had been bragging to her about her and Charlie's relationship, specifically gloating about how much she claimed her girls approved of her sex offender boyfriend. "I'm gonna throw it in Sumi's face and prove that he and others were all wrong about Charlie!" is what Michelle told me Kim had said, but most disturbing of all, was the fact that Kim then reportedly told Michelle that Charlie was planning to move in with her and the girls as early as Wednesday and that Charlie's PO had supposedly approved of this living arrangement.

Naturally, I immediately called the CPS investigator back and updated her on this brand new information. Fortunately, she answered her phone and assured me that CPS would look into the escalating situation. I then also called Dave's brother Nathan to update him as well. Only this time around, Nathan's wife first answered the phone and then had Nathan call me back. Upon hearing shortly after that from Nathan, he now appeared to have changed his attitude toward me somewhat from just the day before. "Look, there's nothing I can do if Charlie's gonna move in with them," he surprised me by dryly stating. "My wife doesn't like that you're calling here about this matter, and our kids are getting concerned about their cousins Lisa and Laura. I do believe you are doing a good thing, a darn good thing, but now we must leave it up to Dave and let him take action alone."

I was a little put off by Nathan's change in demeanor on Sunday, as I had merely wanted to give him the latest information so that he could relay it back to Dave. After all, if these were my nieces in this awful situation, I would definitely want to be given a heads up in advance about Charlie attempting to move in with them. Still, I made sure to remain very polite toward Nathan and be respectful of his wishes. I did not want to do anything to upset anyone in Dave's family, as I knew they were the girls' only hope in this matter. I also understood that the sentiment expressed today had not really come from Nathan, and was not intended to criticize my efforts. I learned that when families are involved in such complicated matters, the reactions can vary greatly from one person to another.

Luckily for Lisa and Laura, I would soon get a glimpse of some positive changes.

Chapter Twenty
Glimpse of Some Positive Changes

Ironically, it was right after this stress-filled weekend that Joan returned from her ten-day trip. With Kim's neighbor back in town, it wasn't long before I would get a new update from Joan on the Charlie situation. On Monday, March 18, I received a phone call from Joan at about 10:50 p.m., and the news she had to share with me was nothing short of a bombshell. Joan informed me that she had observed a sheriff serving Kim with legal documents at 9:30 p.m. that evening!

I was of course elated at hearing this news, as I guessed this was likely the paperwork that Nathan had told me Dave was planning to file by that day. Joan said she observed the sheriff entering Kim's home carrying a big manila envelope and had remained inside for about ten minutes. As the sheriff was leaving, Joan had gone outside to ask him whether there had been any trouble in the neighborhood. "He told me that he had just served Kim with legal papers," she said in relaying his response.

In spite of this seemingly positive information, I still wanted to make sure that Dave's mother was aware of what happened over the weekend, specifically the terrible risk her granddaughters had been subjected to by Kim allowing Charlie to spend overnights. So, on Wednesday, March 20, I sent Kathy an email at 1:46 p.m. updating her on the situation. In doing so, I gave her the name and contact info for the family law attorney whom I had met with in early February to discuss the Charlie matter. I hoped that my email would encourage her and Dave to continue with what they were doing.

Along with reaching out to Kathy on Wednesday afternoon, I then left a voicemail message with the assistant of the judge to whom I had sent a long letter. At 3:48 p.m., the assistant called me back with an encouraging update. She informed me that the judge had indeed received my letter, and had actually been reviewing it earlier that day.

Incredibly, still more positive information would soon be coming my way. Later Wednesday evening, I learned from Joan that little Laura had apparently been visited at her school during recess by a local sheriff. Joan had obtained this information from the mother of one of Laura's young friends. According to what Laura told her young friend, a sheriff and another unidentified woman, likely the CPS investigator, had taken Laura aside and asked her whether Charlie had recently spent an overnight at Laura's home. After so many weeks of urging the legal system to take action, it appeared as though they were finally responding to the call. A sheriff questioning Laura about Charlie only reinforced my long-held belief that this predatory offender was **'not'** allowed anywhere near female minors!

Within the next twenty-four hours, I would soon have the unexpected pleasure of hearing directly from Laura. On the evening of Thursday, March 21, Laura sent me a text message and we communicated back and forth for a bit. While we simply engaged in silly talk, I resisted the impulse to ask her about what had gone on with the sheriff. At any rate, it was a real joy to hear from a child that I had now missed for so long.

Rather than slow down my efforts, a glimpse of some positive changes merely prompted me to do more. On Friday, March 22, I sent a short follow-up letter to the judge informing him about what had happened over the weekend. I felt it was wise to send this brief update, to make the judge aware of Charlie's recent contact with the children and Kim's plans to have him move in, but as it turned out, it wouldn't be the judge, the police, or CPS who would make a lasting impact. Instead, the girls' family would have to step up and finally come to the aid of the children.

On Sunday, March 24, 2013, I received the news I thought I might never hear. At 6:49 p.m. that evening, I got an email from a family law attorney now reportedly representing the girls' father Dave. This wonderful message read as follows:

"Mr. Mukherjee,

I have been retained by Dave concerning the safety of his daughters. I understand that you have been concerned that they have come into contact with a sex offender. Will you please contact me at (phone number given) to discuss your concerns and observations? Thank you kindly."

Naturally, I could not have been more pleased and gratified upon receiving this correspondence. I immediately informed my family and Joan and rejoiced over what had occurred. However, at the very same time, I remained apprehensive and nervous over what would be coming next.

On Tuesday, March 26, Joan and I were both informed by Dave's lawyer's office that we had each been subpoenaed, meaning required to soon testify as witnesses in court, over the Charlie matter on the morning of Monday, April 1. That same afternoon, I spoke on the phone for about forty minutes with an assistant of Dave's lawyer, and filled her in on all of my observations and concerns regarding Lisa and Laura's well-being.

Later that evening, I received an interesting phone call from my friend and ally Joan. Fearful of retaliation from Kim in response to this court proceeding, Joan had visited the local courthouse to inquire about something and happened to ask a clerk to view the police report from the January 20 incident when the cops were first called to Kim's house. Amazingly, she was then told that the police report had been sent to a prosecutor for possible charges. Just as uplifting, was the brief conversation Joan also had with the same officer who responded to that January 20 call. In sharp contrast to how the local police had viewed the situation in early February, this officer now told Joan that Charlie's no longer allowed at Kim's house! While I didn't have any proof as to what had caused these positive changes, I theorized that my note to the judge may indeed have made an impact.

Over the next few days, Joan and I continued to respond to the demands accompanied with the lawyer's subpoenas. These included turning over to the court any email correspondences and/or Facebook/text messages that showed evidence of the girls' contact with Charlie. For my part, I submitted the Facebook message in which Kim encouraged little Laura to send Charlie a valentine, as well as the email Kim sent me on February 3, where she put in writing that Charlie had been at her house and playing a board game with her girls that Saturday night. I also submitted to the court a more recent Facebook message I had received from Kim, in which she bragged to me about how her girls supposedly "loved and adored" her relationship with the convicted child molester. Having made it this far, I wanted to give Dave's lawyer whatever she needed to make her case strong.

Remarkably, while Joan and I were preparing for court, we soon learned that Dave's lawyer was out of the office and on vacation all week; but on Sunday, March 31, which was Easter Sunday and the day before the court hearing, I was finally able to connect by phone with this lady. Even though I had previously disclosed everything to her assistant, I went on to personally fill Dave's lawyer in on all of my concerns and observations. This conversation was essential, as I learned that I would be her star witness the next morning in court. "You are the star witness and the one with the most knowledge in this matter, even more knowledge than my own client Dave," the lawyer told me.

Beyond that, she was not able to give me a lot of information about what would actually happen the next day, other than instructing me that I had to be there in court at 9 a.m. sharp. "The hearing might be postponed, it might be just fifteen minutes, or it might be a full trial of up to three hours," was what she informed me. She also explained that Dave was attempting to obtain court orders to ensure his daughters' personal safety, although she could not elaborate much further than that.

Nervous as I was, it had finally come down to the moment of truth in this matter. I would soon have to face my former friend Kim and see this thing through to the end. Little did I realize as I went to bed that night that Charlie would be in court as well.

Chapter Twenty-one
The Family Finally Takes Action

It was a combination of nervousness and excitement that consumed me on Monday, April 1, 2013, as my dad and I drove out to the courthouse near Kim's neighborhood for the hearing. Upon arriving there around 9 a.m., we met up with Joan and her oldest son, Matt, a curious high school junior who insisted on coming to view the proceedings.

It didn't take me long to observe that I wasn't the only one feeling anxious on this particular morning. My poor friend Joan, a fellow witness in this case, was truly a nervous wreck! With her hands shaking in anticipation, Joan began writing out what she was going to say in court on scratch paper and kept asking me for clarification on the dates of key events in the Charlie matter. Having met briefly outside the courtroom with Dave's lawyer, the four of us (my father, Matt, Joan, and I) were then directed to enter the room with the judge and be seated.

Once in the courtroom, it didn't take me long to quickly spot Kim sitting on a nearby bench. However, I was shocked when I then noticed none other than convicted child molester Charlie Jones sitting right beside her! After alerting my dad to Charlie's presence, I informed Joan of this as well. Joan and I then took further notice of the fact that his mother, who once worked for our state's judicial system, was also present in their corner. We were able to recognize this older woman from pictures we had each viewed of her on Charlie's Facebook page.

The courtroom experience was a somewhat weird and confusing one. The hearing room we were in was quite large and accommodated different groups of people who were there for separate, unrelated legal matters, apparently, all to be heard individually before the very same judge. In other words, we would have to patiently sit and wait for our turn to come.

Though I first assumed that Charlie had come along merely to provide support for Kim, I would soon learn the real reason for his presence in the courtroom. Interestingly on a TV screen monitor, I observed that the girls' father had brought a legal case against Kim as well as one against Charlie. Therefore, Charlie had also received a subpoena and been required to be there on that day. Joan soon informed me that she'd observed Charlie carrying a thick binder full of what appeared to be legal papers. It seemed as though the stage was set for quite a showdown indeed!

Ironically, as it turned out, we would miss most of the action. After reporting our presence to the judge in court, Dave's lawyer instructed both Joan and me to leave the room and wait right outside in the hallway. While my dad followed us out; Joan's son, Matt, remained in the courtroom with Dave's lawyer; Kim; and Charlie. It was certainly an awkward moment when Kim and I had briefly locked eyes, as my former friend initially seemed surprised at seeing me there in the court. As I waited outside with Joan and my dad, Joan remained extremely nervous and kept writing down what she was planning to say when and if called in as a witness. Before long, we all observed Dave and his mother, Kathy, arrive and enter the courtroom.

Remarkably, we would get our update on what was going on inside from none other than Joan's seventeen-year-old son. Several minutes after being asked to wait in the hall, Joan's son, Matt, emerged from the courtroom and told us what had occurred. "Dave's lawyer laid out a strong case and Kim appeared quite nervous," he told us. "The matter was quickly resolved. The judge decided Charlie is not allowed contact with Kim and the girls for one year."

Though Matt's short-term memory of these events was somewhat foggy, he did say that he recalled the judge stating that

Charlie and Kim were not even allowed to text message one another. Naturally, Joan and I were quite pleased with what we had heard. In spite of all of Joan's nervousness, we did not have to testify.

If we might have felt robbed of the full court experience, we would at least get to observe the immediate aftermath. Moments after hearing from Matt, the courtroom doors popped open and Charlie and Kim soon emerged. "I think they're coming out now," I quickly alerted Joan.

"Okay, we better not look at them!" Joan fired back in response.

Unlike Joan who looked down, I decided to face the embattled pair as they walked through the double doors. Interestingly, Kim had a look of defeat and resignation on her face in the form of a little forced smile. Charlie Jones, on the other hand, glared at me with rage in his eyes.

"That's the angry stare that I chose to avoid," Joan said when I shared this with her.

After the two walked away, Dave's lawyer instructed Joan and me to go downstairs and meet with the CPS intake officer to reiterate all our concerns. Upon doing so, we once again shared all the facts and observations with CPS. I particularly placed focus on what had most recently occurred over the weekend of March 15 - 17, with Kim allowing Charlie to spend overnights while Joan was on vacation. The intake officer said CPS would reopen an investigation, and consider the possibility of violating Charlie's probation.

Unlike during our earlier conversations, at this meeting. the intake officer informed us that the CPS investigator had more power than Charlie's PO, and could choose on her own to violate his probation. Along with this information, the intake officer fully validated Joan's and my long-held concerns about him. "It is clear to us what Charlie's intentions are toward Kim's daughters, and we can see how he's been trying to groom them from the start," the intake officer stated. Naturally, Joan and I were both grateful for this comment from CPS.

With all our important work done, there was one more thing I felt I needed to do before leaving the courthouse that morning. After observing Dave's lawyer speaking at length with both Dave and Kathy, I introduced myself to the pair and shook both their hands. This was the one and only time I had ever met Dave, and he appeared quite polite and soft-spoken when I walked up and said hello. The brief greeting was my way of expressing my thanks that the family had finally stepped up.

Not only had they taken action, but as my dad observed, Dave had been quite attentive and interested in the day's proceedings. "Based on what we've heard about Dave, I was concerned that he might not have been able to concentrate or focus well on the hearing," my dad stated, "but on the contrary, he appeared very focused, determined, and involved in everything that happened." I, of course, agreed with my dad's observations and was very impressed with both Dave and Kathy for doing the right thing for the girls!

Later that same afternoon, Joan forwarded me an email message she had received from Dave's lawyer, which clearly explained the outcome of the proceedings we had attended. Along with informing us that the parties had settled this matter, Dave's lawyer specifically shared with us the details of what was determined:

> "A Harassment Restraining Order was entered against Mr. Jones for twelve months. He cannot have contact with the children or come to Kim's home for any reason whatsoever. If you see him there, you can call 911. An Order for Protection was also granted and it prohibits Kim from allowing Charlie Jones to have any contact with the children or coming to the home. It also appoints a Guardian

Ad Litem, and he/she will contact you in the
future."

Naturally, I could not have been more gratified upon
receiving this confirmation. Thanks to my doing the background
check and everything else that had followed, Lisa and Laura were
safe at last from the possible grasp of this convicted child molester.

Chapter Twenty-two
After Our Big Day in Court

It is an uncharacteristically cold weekend night in mid-May 2013, as I stroll into a local Walmart store with young friends Mark, Mike and Tim at my side. While in there, we do all the same old things that we've always done on such outings; search the store for items, joke and tease one another, and eventually pressure the kid who can't decide what he's wanting to buy; but unfortunately, as I push our shopping cart down the various aisles of the store, it is much lighter now than it once used to be. This is sadly the case because the two who were accustomed to riding in that cart are no longer with us today.

Even with the passage of time, I continue to feel the loss of Lisa and Laura from my life. There is definitely a gaping void there, and an empty space that cannot be filled by anyone else. While the laughter, joy, and fond memories will always remain in my heart, I long once again to see the two girls who created so many of these.

After our big day in court, there appeared to be an opportunity for reconciliation between Kim and me. However sadly, I found the offer to be a hollow one after reading the fine print. On the evening of Sunday, April 14, 2013, I had suddenly received an unexpected text message from Kim. In it, she amazingly apologized to me for everything that had happened, and went on to acknowledge that she apparently now understood that I was only looking out for her best interest in everything that I had done.

However, this alleged "apology" also came along with a shrewd demand. In the same message, she then asked me to testify against her ex-husband Dave in upcoming court proceedings regarding their children. "Please be sure to stress in court of what the girls have told you about their father and what you know of him," Kim insisted. In saying this, I knew that she was referring to when her girls had once told us they'd found pornography in the closet at Dave's apartment, along with wrapped condoms in his kitchen drawer. There had also been times that the girls had complained of smelling marijuana in his place, along with saying that he apparently did not feed them well on some occasions.

Though I would certainly attest to these statements made by the girls if asked in court about Dave, I wasn't intending to volunteer any negative info about him. Although Dave did likely have some issues, in my opinion, they simply did not compare with the risks to which Kim had subjected their daughters. While her message might have provided me an attempt at regaining her friendship, I decided it would be best for me to not respond in this instance.

Along with hearing from Kim in mid-April, I would later be contacted as well by Dave's attorney. In fact, about a month later, on Monday, May 13, while returning home from a business trip, I received an email from the lawyer who was representing Dave. She asked for my continued help as a witness with filling out an affidavit for court. Incredibly, she said the paperwork was due back signed and notarized the following afternoon before 4 p.m. In addition to not giving me prior notice, I quickly observed that much of her two-page write up was littered with factual errors. Worst of all was the fact that she did not even remember little Laura's name correctly!

Over the following day, I rewrote the lawyer's entire affidavit and then showed it to her for review. After she expressed her gratitude and further commented that my rewrite was "very well worded," I was able to sign the document and have it notarized at my bank. I was then able to fax it back to the lawyer ahead of the 4 p.m. deadline, on Tuesday, May 14, 2013. Below is the actual affidavit, with some necessary changes made to the actual names of the people:

*I am Sumi Mukherjee. I used to be in a relationship with Kim. We remained friends after our relationship ended.

*I contacted Joan who then contacted Dave's family and informed them of Mr. Jones' criminal background after I became aware of it.

*I checked Mr. Jones' criminal background after I had observed Kim exposing Lisa and Laura to what appeared to be grooming behavior by an adult male in her household on December 31, 2012. I attended a New Year's Eve Party at her home.

*At the party, Kim's male friend was making repeated attempts to touch both girls in a manner that made me uncomfortable. He caressed their hair with his fingers, rubbed ten-year-old Laura's lower backside with his foot and grabbed and tickled thirteen-year-old Lisa repeatedly. Lisa was being flirtatious and tickling the man's upper thigh area by squeezing it and running away, and Kim sat on the couch and verbally encouraged this behavior, specifically urging the man to chase after Lisa and tickle her, saying "Go Rick! Go get her! You have my permission!" With Kim's encouragement and urging, Lisa then continued her role in these flirtatious interactions and the man (Rick) then escalated his role as well.

*On Saturday, January 19, 2013, I told Kim all about Mr. Jones' criminal history as a convicted child molester and registered predatory offender toward young girls.

*Because Kim exhibited such inappropriate bad judgment where this prior individual Rick was concerned, I became concerned and suspicious and then had my lawyer look up Mr. Jones when she posted on Facebook two weeks later that she was now dating him. My lawyer discovered Mr. Jones' criminal history and disclosed this to me on January 17, and I then gathered all the online records I could find to use to warn Kim about the risks her daughters would be facing on January 19.

*When I brought this confirmed information to the attention of Kim, she dismissed it as being untrue and, according to eyewitnesses Joan and Michelle, Kim continued to allow predatory offender Mr. Jones around her daughters and at their home for overnights. That is specifically why I then contacted a sexual assault phone hotline worker, child protection, and eventually Dave's family. I felt that Dave, as a father, should know about the danger his daughters were in with predatory offender Mr. Jones spending time around them.

As it turned out, it appears as though my affidavit likely had a positive impact on the situation. On the morning of Monday, June 3, 2013, I was contacted by Joan and for once, she had what was overall wonderful news to share with me. Although Kim now had yet another new boyfriend in her life, Joan told me she had spoken with the girls' father Dave on Sunday, June 2, as he was bringing the girls back to Kim's house in the evening. Joan said Dave had told her that he was well aware of Kim's latest partner, as Kim was now required to provide Dave with the name, date of birth, and social security number of any new man whom she's dating! Naturally, Dave told Joan this information would allow him to do his own background check on the new person.

137

Dave had also informed her that he had recently been granted more parenting time with his daughters. He assured Joan that he had plenty of support from others with what he was doing, and that people were supposedly watching over Kim and monitoring her behavior. Joan also mentioned that she had observed Kim's parents giving her rides once again, now that she and Charlie were over. During the time when they'd been together, Joan had told me she had persistently observed Kim getting her daily rides from a female friend only, as her own parents had apparently cut her off while she had been dating Charlie.

As you probably could have guessed by now, I still remained somewhat worried about this brand new guy in Kim and her daughters' lives. According to Joan, in June 2013, he was already spending overnights at Kim's house with her daughters present. While this guy might not have a criminal record, Kim's judgment in allowing guys like Rick and Charlie around leaves me concerned about her daughters' well-being. In sharing this news with a friend, he reminded me that I cannot allow such fears to take over my existence. "You can't let yourself obsess about this stuff, Sumi, or else it will give you a heart attack," he warned me.

I immediately remembered that is exactly the same advice Joan had given me earlier, and it helped to have this opinion reinforced. I also knew in my heart that the girls' lives were better today due to my many deeds. Nonetheless, while I agree it's true I cannot let it take over my life, I do feel there is reason to maintain a level of concern for these girls and their plight.

The text messages from the girls have stopped over time, and I am heartbroken to report that as of spring 2013, neighbor boys Mark and Mike have informed me that the girls supposedly did not like me anymore. Anytime that I've seen the boys since mid-January, I would always tell them to let the girls know I still loved them and missed them a lot. When the boys delivered these messages, they said both girls would respond with indifference and verbally claim they no longer liked me. While I'm guessing that Kim's influence could be affecting her daughters' perspective, it still hurts me to imagine that our special bond no longer exists. Writing this book, in a way, has helped me to feel a connection with them by sharing their story. I hope that one day they will understand that I just wanted them to be safe, and hopefully, someday their mother Kim will understand that as well.

Whenever I feel down and miss them and feel as though I've lost them forever, I try hard to remind myself what my feisty girls would likely say to me in such a difficult situation. Along with assuring me that in their hearts they still loved me, they would probably utter the few simple words that would bring a smile back to my face:

"Don't be a dumbass and a pussy now, Dad. You know that you'll see us again!"

Chapter Twenty-three

What We Can All Learn From This Story

As you know well by now, this book has no shortage of riveting drama, suspense, humor, and heartfelt emotion. Not to mention being filled with seemingly bizarre and unusual situations. Catchy and interesting as these factors may be, they are not the reason why I decided to write this book. It is also important to note that while the book honestly reveals my raw emotions throughout this misadventure, I never intended to use the book as a means by which to exploit the lives of others; to say negative things about my former close friend, Kim; or to judge her overall character based on decisions she has made in her life.

Rather, I firmly believe there is something that we, as citizens and human beings, can all learn from this most unique story, and that the public can benefit greatly from the important lessons herein. That is why I felt it necessary to write this book, while carefully protecting the identities of the actual persons involved. Over the course of this final chapter, I will summarize what I feel we can and should all take with us after reading Father Figure.

Silent Victims

I have a very important message for every child reading this who is currently suffering in silence from sexual abuse, and it has to do with secrets. Even though I was fortunate enough to not experience sexual abuse in my life, I feel as though I have a unique understanding and appreciation for what those of you who are experiencing it are currently going through.

This is because I, just like you, have spent a significant period of my life concealing a terrifying secret from everyone. From the ages of sixteen to twenty-one, I suffered in silence each and every day of my existence. Though my secret wasn't sexual abuse, it was living with a mental illness that I believed would destroy my future if revealed to anyone. Though I was suffering in silence with the symptoms of severe OCD, I didn't know what was wrong with me and honestly believed that I was going insane, and with my mother herself being a licensed psychologist, I was haunted by the irony of how this could possibly be happening to someone like me!

Worst of all, I was certain that if my parents ever learned about the bizarre obsessive thoughts I was having and the bizarre things (compulsive behaviors) that I was doing, that I would immediately be committed to a mental institution where I would spend the rest of my life. Not only would I have lost my freedom, but I imagined that everyone I knew would then become aware that I had gone crazy and had been sent to the nuthouse. I feared I would be spending my days locked in a rubber room by myself, all alone. There would be no friends, no girlfriends, no college, no job, and no future for me whatsoever. This fear was so intense and paralyzing that I kept my mouth shut and told no one. No one. Not for five miserably long years of my youth.

Those years spent living as a silent victim, were by far the worst years of my life. Every day I was petrified that someone would learn my secret, and that whatever few joys I had left would be taken from me. Yet, at the same time, part of me prayed every day that another living soul would somehow learn what was happening to me and would help me. Those five years felt more like five thousand to me. I thought I would never survive.

My experience of concealing my mental illness for five years has given me a sense of appreciation for what others must go through, who have also been forced to live a long time with a secret; whatever that secret may be. From what I've read and understood of CSA, the feeling a silent victim experiences seems quite similar to mine.

At the age of twenty-one, I finally broke my long silence and told my parents. I only did so, however, because the symptoms of my mental illness had become so terrible that they caused me to resign from my job. I could barely function at all, and finally felt that being sent to a mental hospital wouldn't be any worse than what my life had already become. That threat was no longer valid. So, at last, I decided to talk.

While my own experiences have given me a general idea of living with a secret, I still do not know firsthand how it actually feels to live with sexual abuse as a child. I can only imagine how awful, confusing, frightening, and uncomfortable it must be for those of you who do. I imagine you must feel shame and guilt as well, although you certainly do not deserve to. I try to imagine how I would feel if my abuser was someone whom I loved dearly, such as a parent, a parent's partner, a family member, a teacher, a close friend, a coach, or a priest. I try to imagine how I would feel if the abuser was someone on whom I depended for shelter and money. Regardless of who the abuser may be, I know it would be really bad.

I have read about how abusers often use guilt trips to keep children silent, or even threaten to harm the child, the child's pets, the child's loved ones, or to even harm themselves. Just as daunting, I've also read how abusers may tell the child to remain silent to keep the family's positive image in the eyes of others, or to simply keep the family from breaking apart. It would also be incredibly difficult if the abuser is someone who your family loves and respects and depends on. No matter what the situation may be, they most often will try to use guilt trips and threats.

To all of the silent victims reading Father Figure, I want you to see that there are some adults like me who do love and care about children. There are some adults like me who would do whatever it takes to help you with what you are living with, no matter how awful or hopeless it seems. You have seen how I did that for the kids in this true story. I have loved so many kids in my life, and none of them have even been my own flesh and blood, but I genuinely care about children, and there are others like me who do too.

I am asking you, right here and now, to find the courage you possess to tell someone about what is happening to you. To this day I don't know for certain if sexual abuse has happened to Lisa, but based upon what I observed I fear that it likely did happen. If so, there is nothing in the world that I was able to do to prevent it before I met Lisa and entered her life. Now sadly, I am no longer a part of her life, but maybe, if some of you read Father Figure and decide now to ask for help, then perhaps I am able to help end the nightmare for you.

I would encourage you to try and tell someone whom you trust if you're being abused. If you don't know of any such person in your life, you can do what I did and reach out to a sexual assault crisis phone hotline worker. Betty, the lady I spoke to, was one of the most gentle and caring individuals I have ever interacted with in my thirty-seven years of life. There are others like her who would listen to you if you approached them. These days, all it takes is using the search terms 'sexual assault crisis phone hotline' on Google to find such a number in your area. If you don't have internet access, there is always using the phone book, going to the library, or asking someone who does in some form.

School is another excellent place to speak out, as all school employees are required by law to help you if you tell them you are being abused in any way. You may recall how the young girl who Charlie abused told her friend and her school counselor about what had happened, even when she did not tell her own mother! She did the right thing and because of it Charlie was not able to touch her again.

143

If you are a silent victim, you can also feel free to tell me about it. I will likely encourage you to tell a trained professional in your local community who can help you better than I can alone, but I would be happy to provide support as you get through that process. It doesn't matter what your life is like today, or for how long you may have been abused. It doesn't matter if you are a young child or are past your eighteenth birthday. Things can improve and it's well worth your effort. I am not going to lie and tell you that it's going to be easy for you. However, I do believe with all of my heart that you do need to speak up and that in the long run, it will be so worthwhile.

No matter what you may have done in your life or what mistakes you have made, **nobody deserves to be abused!** Maybe you have never felt loved by anyone, or ever been told that you are a worthy person who does not deserve to be abused. If that is the case, let me be the first person to tell you that now. Although I haven't been lucky enough to meet you, I already care about you and want your life to get better. You are why I have written this book! It doesn't matter what your abuser may have told you, or how many times they have said it. Believe me when I say that it is never a victim's fault. You deserve to have control over yourself and your own body, and no one, not even a loved one, has the right to take that from you.

Along these same lines, it is important for children to know that they are **'never'** responsible for how reporting abuse may make an adult feel. A female friend of mine, now twenty-three years of age, recently told me about how her mother's current boyfriend had frequently touched her inappropriately back when she was a teenager. This abuse usually occurred whenever she would be getting out of the shower. Along with telling me that she had never told anyone else about this, my friend further stated that she didn't tell her mother because she felt responsible for how her mother might feel if informed about the abuse. "My mother already had so many failed relationships, and I felt bad about telling her because I feared it would likely result in her losing yet another boyfriend."

Though we all know it is good practice to be thoughtful toward the feelings of others, there are some circumstances in life where it is both okay and necessary to be focused on yourself. Telling an adult that you are being abused is a circumstance where it is crucial for a child to speak up, and to not feel responsible for the impact they fear this information may have on the adult(s) that they share it with. Doing so can not only save yourself, but can potentially save the lives of many other children as well. In this particular case, my female friend also told me there are new children entering into the lives of her mother and boyfriend today, and now these children may be at risk for similar abuse by the boyfriend as well. Even if feelings are hurt and relationships are broken, it is always far better in the long run that children report being abused to adults.

I once read a beautiful, very realistic quote by Mary Anne Radmacher that stated, "Courage does not always roar. Sometimes, it is the quiet voice at the end of the day that says I will try again tomorrow." There is always another tomorrow. If you are a silent victim, please choose to break your silence and to reach out to someone for help. I hope and pray that Father Figure will motivate you toward taking that step.

Caregivers of Children

Though much of the advice in this section is addressed to single mothers, it is also essential and applicable information for all caregivers of children. I am using the term "caregivers" here to include all parents, guardians, foster parents, relatives and others who look after kids. Therefore, I request all who care for children to please read through this section as well.

According to the book, "Identifying Child Molesters" by Carla Van Dam, many molesters specifically target children with single parents, and as you have read, Father Figure is filled with

145

many important lessons for single mothers. The most prominent of these is that single mothers must get to know a man carefully **before** they introduce him to their children. So too, must a single mom get to know a man well **before** she gives him personal information about her children. In making this point, I now ask you to recall the second chapter of this book. This is where I discuss my first meeting with Kim, and how she told me all about her girls and then showed me several pictures of them. Obviously, in my case, Kim's decision to do this turned out to be a safe one, but single mothers have no way of knowing up front whether they are getting a good man like me, or someone with bad intentions.

Since this will naturally be unknown in the beginning stages of contact, I recommend that single moms do not give new men a lot of information about their children. For example, within my first few meetings with Kim, I knew so much about her young daughters, including their issues with their father and what schools they each attended. Both of these pieces of information make the girls vulnerable to a new man with the *wrong* intentions. Knowing right away that there is strain in the girls' relationship with their father, tells a new man that these children may be easier for him to manipulate. Also telling the man what schools they attend can be risky.

One of the main reasons I decided to tell Kim's girls about Charlie when I confronted Kim, is because I feared he already knew which schools they attended, and that he might show up one day at their schools and tell them, falsely, that their mom had been in a terrible accident. At that point, I was afraid he might try to lure them to go somewhere with him, presumably to see their mom at the hospital. If this deceptive move was successful, the harm done to a child could be irreversible!

Showing pictures of one's children to a new man is also not advisable, especially the one Kim showed me of her girls taking a bath together. Can you imagine how a convicted child molester might react to viewing such a revealing photo? I shudder to think if he was also shown that same picture by Kim. If so, it could have served to make him aware that this mother was likely naïve in regards to her children's personal safety. Though being targeted by a predator is never a single mom's fault, this awareness can certainly help her to protect her kids even more.

I would recommend that a single mother do a background check on a man before introducing him to her children. Had a background check not been done by me on Charlie, years might have gone by without anyone knowing what he was convicted of doing to children. The importance of doing a background check is clearly established in Father Figure. Once again, I do not at all regret meeting Kim's girls shortly after I met her. However, until a lady gets to know a man well and does a background check, she should not introduce him to her children. Coming from a man myself, any man worth meeting your children would respect the precautions you choose to take. Be wary of those who appear too eager to meet and spend time with your kids.

I fully respect and understand that like all people, single mothers have sexual desires. If a single mom tries out relationship possibilities with new men, this should occur outside of the home and without the children's involvement. If such meetings do occur at the woman's house, the children should not be present when this happens. Again, this point is strongly made in Father Figure when Kim invited Rick over. Although New Year's Eve was presumably their first meeting, Kim allowed Rick to drink heavily enough to pass out and to spend the night with her daughters present. She obviously did not know Rick well enough, and he clearly didn't think enough of her to even reply to her text the next day. Such one night encounters should not occur in the presence of children, even if the man isn't outwardly creepy. Exposing the children to many different men who are not well known by the mom increases their risk of experiencing maltreatment. Use of alcohol and drugs during such encounters raises their risk even more.

A single mom should not use her children to help win her partner's affections. This was clearly evidenced in Father Figure, when Kim encouraged her daughter Laura to send Charlie a special card for Valentine's Day. It was also evidenced when Kim seemed to be encouraging flirtatious behavior between her daughter Lisa and Rick. Involving the kids in the relationship should only occur once the woman has known the man very well and has done a background check. In the cases of Rick and Charlie, Kim should not have involved her children at all.

If using online dating websites as Kim was, single mothers should state in their profiles that they must get to know a man well over time before he will meet their children. This precaution would likely discourage predators who are trolling the internet looking for moms in desperate search of a dad for their kids. Knowing it will take them considerable time and effort to meet a lady's children may deter some child molesters. It is also advisable for a single mom not to mention the gender of her children in her dating profile. This move is likely helpful, as child predators usually have a gender preference and may pass a lady by if the gender of her kids is not easily known. I'm guessing Kim likely mentioned in her profile that she was a mom of young daughters. She might have even included some pictures of them. With this information, a predator of young girls would likely know right away that this is where he should focus his efforts.

When and if using online dating websites, single mothers should make sure they keep such activities private from their children. If the children are around at the time, single mothers should establish appropriate boundaries with regards to their children's observance of such activities.

In Father Figure, you may recall how Kim told me she had caught her thirteen-year-old daughter Lisa secretly corresponding with adult males via an online dating website. Lisa reportedly told Kim she had done this, because she had observed Kim doing it and therefore wanted to try it as well. It appears as though Kim did not set clear boundaries and help Lisa understand that it is not safe or appropriate for a minor to correspond on dating websites with grown men! On the contrary, such behavior can result in a minor becoming a victim of sexual abuse.

Single mothers must also remind themselves that their children's best interests must be put ahead of their own. This I felt was a key problem with Kim's approach in Father Figure. In spite of being told about Charlie's criminal history, she did not want to lose this guy and put her own needs for male companionship ahead of her daughters' personal safety. She did so not merely by dating Charlie, but by making her children have contact with this registered predatory offender. I'm not suggesting that single mothers need to sacrifice everything for their children. However, they do need to use good judgment and ensure that their children are not subjected to unnecessary bad risks, as they often were in Father Figure.

If an adult is spending time with your children, caregivers need to talk with their kids and make sure the adult is behaving in a sexually appropriate manner. This is something which Joan told me she had done with her boys, Mark and Mike, whenever they'd stay overnight at my house. Joan and I were, fortunately, close enough where she could openly tell me that she'd asked her boys whether they felt comfortable around me, and whether or not I would maintain appropriate boundaries when in a locker room together, while undressing at bedtime, etc. Joan also informed me that she had gone ahead on her own and done a background check on me. Though Joan was concerned I might feel offended when she told me this, on the contrary, I applauded her decision to communicate openly with her children about their personal safety.

Whether a single mother or not, any caregiver should use this approach whenever their children spend time with a grown up. Making your children aware of appropriate boundaries with adults is quite helpful in preventing sexual abuse. It is, of course, important that the adult caregiver has also acquired the appropriate knowledge about boundaries and understands and has the ability to listen well and respond appropriately to the child. One book that can help adults do this with young children is, "My body belongs to me" by Jill Starishevsky. As was evidenced in Father Figure, Kim seemed far too relaxed when it came to teaching her kids about boundaries. It is children who know nothing about appropriate sexual boundaries that are at an elevated risk for experiencing maltreatment. This was clearly a problem with Lisa and Laura. Though I first found the girls' flirtations toward me to be silly and harmless, I became aware of the risks involved when I saw Lisa flirting with Rick. I, too, have learned from this whole situation. Looking back now, I wish that I had been stricter in response to this kind of behavior.

If a single mother chooses to date a known child molester, then she must do so without ever involving her children or allowing them to meet her date. This statement may come across as common sense to many people, and many would argue that no one should date a known child molester to begin with!

Regardless, I felt the need to specifically mention this as I have run into a similar situation with another very close friend of mine. During this whole episode I experienced with Kim, I happened to learn from this other single mother friend of mine that she, too, had begun dating a convicted child molester. In the case of this woman, her date had pleaded guilty to groping and kissing a little girl once in a public place. Though this woman insisted that the guy had turned himself in and told her about his criminal record on their first date, I still would not recommend dating someone with any history of mistreating kids in a sexual manner.

Having said that, I would like to point out, given her choice to still date him, this woman dealt with the matter much better than my former friend Kim. To begin with, this woman took it upon herself to immediately inform her children's father about her date's criminal history. She also resolved from the start that she would **never** allow her date to meet her two children, until they became adults, no matter how far their relationship may progress.

When I had an opportunity to talk with this woman, I told her about the situation with Kim and asked for her opinion. "Oh, I completely understand why Kim wants to date Charlie," this woman said to me. "She just wants to feel loved, Sumi, and

150

Charlie must be the only person who can make her feel that way."
Hearing from this woman gave me some insight into how Kim
might have felt, and why she might have acted as she did in this
situation.

I want to specifically reach out now to those single mothers,
like Kim and this other woman, who may feel the urge to date a
known child molester or sex offender. My message to you is that
while I don't agree with your decision, I do not fault you for
wanting to be with someone who makes you feel loved. I am also
not going to judge you for your decision. I only ask that you please
do not involve your children and do not allow him to meet them.
That is all I am asking of you. Please follow this woman's good
example, and be sure to keep your kids safe.

If you observe your child acting out with aggression and/or
displaying possible signs of being molested, please be willing to
seek professional help for your child. As you may recall from the
fifth chapter of this book, I have described what appeared to me to
be disturbing behaviors and several possible signs of sexual abuse
in children with regards to Lisa. Tragically, Kim repeatedly
refused to seek help for her daughter. If you find your child in a
similar predicament, I ask you to please take their behaviors
seriously and be willing to get them help. The sooner they get help,
the better off they will be upon entering adulthood. While it may
seem frightening at first to open up to a trained professional, the
benefit to your child over time can be immeasurable, and being a
minor, your child simply cannot choose to get professional help on
their own. They will need your courage and willingness to step
outside of your comfort zone and to take what may feel like a risk
in asking someone for help. In the long run and from my own years
in therapy, I honestly believe the experience will benefit you both.

If a caregiver has experienced sexual abuse in their past, I
recommend they seek counseling so that it does not impact how
they raise their children. In chapter five of Father Figure, you read
how Kim's experiences as a possible victim of sexual abuse might
have impacted the manner in which she raised her young

daughters. Specifically, Kim often shared her twisted belief with her girls that males who are found guilty of sexual misconduct are often innocent, and that females who are victimized merely got what was coming to them. It is exactly this kind of flawed thinking that can discourage children from reporting sexual abuse should they experience it. Perhaps if Kim had gotten therapy for what she had been through, she might not have gone on to instill these wrongful, potentially harmful beliefs in her children. Also, she would have been less likely to believe a convicted child molester easily and to allow him around her young girls. Once again Carla Van Dam's book, "Identifying Child Molesters," backs up this sentiment. "Those who were themselves molested often have difficulty with assertiveness and do not know how to provide their children with the differentiation so necessary for protection from abuse," the book candidly states. "It is no accident that eighty-nine percent of women who were sexually abused themselves as children have children who become victims of sexual abuse as well."

In sharing these tips and advice, it is certainly not my intention to make caregivers feel paranoid about their children's personal safety. However, keeping yourself and your children informed is an excellent way to ensure their well-being.

I hope the many lessons in Father Figure will stick with caregivers who read this.

Ordinary Citizens

If there is one message in this book to ordinary citizens everywhere; it is to fully realize, appreciate and understand the difference that we can each make in the life of a vulnerable child. This is only possible to achieve, of course, when we listen to our gut instinct and then choose to become involved. Right, there are two of the simplest concepts that most people fail to apply on a daily basis. Yet, you can see how they played such key roles here in Father Figure. Oh sure it is nice to jump on the bandwagon when we hear such topics discussed at length on our favorite talk shows, but to follow one's gut and become involved are things that most people don't do.

Why is this so often the case? Well, most of us have busy lives and cannot easily find time to go out of our normal routines for a possible worthy cause. Also, when it comes to issues regarding someone's family, we are raised to believe that families are to be respected and not interfered with. Certainly, people are frowned upon for being nosy and butting into the personal lives of others, let alone daring to question what a parent chooses to do with their own child.

Yet there can be situations, such as described in Father Figure, where interference becomes necessary; as I simply cannot imagine what Lisa and Laura's lives would be like right now if I hadn't chosen to intervene! Based upon what I had observed occurring in these young girls' lives, doing the background check and everything else that followed was certainly warranted, and as you can see from reading Father Figure, the end result speaks for itself.

The biggest reason why most ordinary citizens do not wish to become involved, even when they know it's the right thing to do, is because they often do not understand who to report to, how they will be involved, what will happen if they do, and/or they understandably do not wish to suffer all the distress and repercussions which Joan and I were forced to endure. While I have openly shared how awful the hardships were that we both encountered, including my ultimate loss of Kim and her daughters' friendship, it was definitely well worth going through to try and save the girls from the probable threat to their personal safety. Hopefully, somewhere down the road, maybe years from now, they will understand and they'll thank me. Even if not, their lives are much better today with appropriate court orders in place for their continued safety. It is my foremost hope that Father Figure serves as a heartfelt, inspiring motivation for everyone reading it to also be willing to go to some or similar lengths for vulnerable children in your respective communities.

What happened in this true story **can** and **does** happen more frequently than people realize, and more frequently than any of us would further wish to acknowledge. In this day and age, with technology such as iPhones; the Internet; and Facebook, it is easier than before to take precautions and advocate safety on behalf of the children who we feel are at risk. I implore and challenge everyone reading this to take a moment today to reexamine whether there is a vulnerable child in your community who could possibly benefit from your help and involvement. If so, please find the courage and creativity to try and assist that child, of course with proper attention to the legal system and the laws of our society.

Even when the situation repeatedly felt hopeless in Father Figure, I continued to brainstorm, to think outside the box, and to look for new lawful ways to remain effective. In other words, I simply refused to give up. As a society, our children are our most valuable resources and are quite literally our future. Each one deserves the right to grow up feeling safe and respected, and to grow up in an environment free of all forms of abuse. As the adults, it is our responsibility and obligation to give each precious child that full opportunity. To all ordinary citizens reading this, I hope you will learn from this story.

Family Members

After reading this book, you can see how the girls' family played a key role in ensuring their personal safety. As we learned in Father Figure, biological family members are often the only ones with the legal power to take action on behalf of vulnerable children.

To all people reading this, please keep this story in mind if someone ever advises you that children related to you are in a potentially unsafe situation, and if you do find yourself in such a predicament, I ask that you please act quickly and do not delay becoming involved. In Father Figure, you read how Joan and I had to approach Dave's family multiple times in order for them to take action on behalf of Lisa and Laura. While I fully commend Dave and his family now for what they have accomplished, I was concerned with the length of time it took for them to get moving at first.

While all legal process is time consuming, there were instances where I wish the family could have acted quicker. The major one which comes to mind was when I had spoken over the phone with Kathy, the girls' paternal grandma, in late February 2013. Though she had seemed to understand the urgency during our phone conversation, it appeared to me that she had delayed being involved due to spending time with her friends. Knowing that Kim was allowing that man to spend overnights near her girls, this delay could have possibly given him additional time to prey on the kids.

While I'm relieved to say in this case that it's now water under the bridge, families do need to take swift action with the welfare of children at stake, whether the possible threat is coming from outside of or within the family. It is possible that family members might face some of the inconsistent or unsatisfactory responses that Joan and I had to deal with, but it is also true that the 'family' connection can give them a better chance at succeeding as compared to ordinary citizens in a situation like this when the possible threat is not coming from an existing family member. It can, however, be more difficult for family members to report and to get appropriate responses if the threat is from within the family. As per Dr. Pamela Pine, PhD, MPH, Founder and CEO, Stop the Silence: Stop Child Sexual Abuse, Glenn Dale, MD, "There can be increased issues in systems responses when a family member reports, also due to various factors such as a reluctance to believe or the desire not to believe that a father (for example), is capable of doing something like this to his child; and a lack of understanding by those presiding over various systems (e.g., courts, police, social services) about the intricacies of CSA, the high likelihood of children's reports, the dynamics inside the family when a report of CSA is made about a family member, and other factors."

Law Enforcement

Perhaps the greatest mystery remaining from Father Figure, and the leading cause of our setbacks in this story, is the confusing reactions that we received from the police in Kim's town. Though this appeared to finally change after I wrote to the judge, I can never forget how helpless I felt when we were apparently let down by the cops.

To this day, I remain utterly confused over what actually happened behind the scenes with law enforcement. From the outside looking in, it seemed as though they were plagued with discrepancies over how they should deal with Charlie. This appeared quite evident on January 20, the first time the cops were called out to Kim's house. Given the reaction from CPS, and the eventual consensus by the local police, it seems as though Charlie should **not** have been allowed anywhere near minor girls.

To law enforcement officers reading this, I request that you please use this most unique story as a case study for similar situations in the future and encourage your units to support more training in handling cases of CSA. In a similar predicament concerning a sex offender, I certainly hope that law enforcement will err on the side of caution and choose to protect the kids. I also hope that a citizen will not feel threatened by law enforcement when he/she is reporting a good faith concern. Regardless of what rules or regulations were in place at the time, there was no justification that we could see for the local police to threaten Joan like they did. We believe that we had approached law enforcement with a very good faith concern, and nothing that Joan or I did had warranted such an aggressive response. In general we felt there was a lack of swift and appropriate response to the reported threat.

I have always had the highest regard for the law enforcement profession. However, I must admit that for many months after this situation, I had a very negative feeling toward police officers in general. Every time I saw a cop car drive by, I had a bitter taste in my mouth. Over time, I have worked with myself to instead focus on all the great officers who dedicate their lives to serve and protect us each day. Law enforcement is still one of the most honorable professions.

To all officers reading this story, please continue to restore my faith. Please use this story to do your best to look out for those children at risk.

CPS

In spite of the apparent lack of support from local law enforcement at the time, I am grateful that CPS still took an interest in investigating this matter. One of the biggest lessons I learned through this ordeal is more about how CPS works in our country.

Due to the nature of privacy laws, it is difficult sometimes to be sure that CPS will react in a fully protective manner or to get updates on your case after you have made your initial report to CPS. As you know from reading Father Figure, I often struggled with not hearing back from the person handling the investigation. I also felt frustrated when I was told that this case was a lower priority, simply because CPS had to wait for something more to occur.

There are a number of places where CPS in our country needs some changes. There needs to be greater focus placed on truly **preventing** a likely hazard, just as there is in responding to one that has already occurred. I am also disappointed that given all they knew, CPS did not choose to violate Charlie's probation after our meeting of April 1.

I know that the vast majority of CPS workers are dedicated to this cause and that in spite of the systemic shortcomings, CPS did take some constructive actions and provided support to Dave and his mother. Their guidance was likely essential in encouraging Dave to become more involved.

In summary, we need to do better in this area. According to Dr. Pamela Pine, Founder and CEO, Stop the Silence: Stop Child Sexual Abuse, Glenn Dale, MD, "There are many instances when reporting a case of suspected or known CSA can wind up in a morass or non-response or worse. As with Law Enforcement, there are often problems too with respect to CPS not having enough training on CSA or a full enough understanding of situations surrounding it. CPS management and workers, as well as members of the police, should be required to attend a solid training on the issue of CSA – how it happens, why it happens, who the offenders likely are, how to detect the possibility of it occurring, its impact, how to handle possible cases, etc".

To all CPS staff members reading this, please use this story as a reminder on the importance of preventive action in keeping our children safer. I applaud all the good work you do.

Department of Corrections

Along with the response from law enforcement, the other mystery remaining from Father Figure is the reaction of Charlie's PO and the DOC.

According to the CPS intake officer, it was Charlie's PO who was allowing him to spend overnights near Kim's young daughters. If true as stated, this goes in sharp contrast to what most of us believe a PO's duties are when supervising a child molester. Given Charlie's criminal history with children (committing the act overnight), his two prior probation violations and the restrictions imposed by the sentencing judge, this predatory offender should not have been cleared to spend overnights near any children!

Furthermore, I was deeply disappointed by the apparent lack of care and follow up from the DOC supervisor, who was the boss of this PO. In spite of my detailed letter and phone call, it appears that the supervisor failed to look into the matter and take actions to ensure the girls' personal safety. I did not receive any specific feedback from her that would confirm to me that this matter was ever addressed.

Regardless of these negative experiences, I continue to have enough faith in our legal system and the correction system to believe that what happened here might have been due to some unusual circumstances that I am not fully aware of. I believe in most cases POs and supervisors do handle situations like these appropriately, using their job training, common sense, and good judgment. To all POs and DOC staff members reading this, I hope that this story can be seen as a practical case study. Please always respect how vulnerable children in these circumstances can be, and look out for their rights and well-being.

Sexual Assault Crisis Counselors

I am quite pleased to say that I could not be more satisfied with the performance by Betty, the sexual assault crisis counselor whom I was fortunate enough to encounter. As I described in Father Figure, she was extremely validating, nurturing, and supportive in her role as a crisis counselor. This is especially noteworthy, as my call was a bit more challenging and complicated than I'm guessing she was used to dealing with on a regular basis.

Even though Betty didn't instantly have all the answers for my unique dilemma, she went the extra mile by continuing to brainstorm ideas long after our call had concluded. Furthermore, she then took it upon herself to contact a CPS officer and personally pave the way for me to report my concerns directly to them while remaining anonymous. She also made the effort to call me back the following day and give me this information. Once again, I wonder whether CPS would have taken any interest in the matter had it not been for Betty contacting them herself first as a crisis counselor. Betty's performance in this difficult situation should serve as a training model for all other rape and sexual assault crisis counselors to learn from.

Whoever you are, a child or an adult; a parent or a nonparent; I thank you for your interest in reading *Father Figure – My Mission to Prevent Child Sexual Abuse*. I truly hope that it has a positive impact in your life and the lives of other people you connect with.

List of Helpful Resources for Preventing Child Sexual Abuse

"Stockholm Syndrome and Child Sexual Abuse" by Shirley Julich, *Journal of Child Sexual Abuse*, 2005, Vol. 14, Issue 3, p 107-129

Stop the Silence: Stop Child Sexual Abuse (www.stopthesilence.org)

RAINN – Rape, Abuse, and Incest National Network (www.rainn.org)

Darkness To Light – a non-profit organization in South Carolina seeking to protect children from sexual abuse (www.d2l.org)

"Identifying Child Molesters – Preventing Child Sexual Abuse by Recognizing the Patterns of the Offenders," by Carla Van Dam, Ph.D.

"The Epidemic of Rape and Child Sexual Abuse in the United States," by Diana E.H. Russell and Rebecca M. Bolen

"My Body Belongs to Me," by Jill Starshevsky

"A Sourcebook on Child Sexual Abuse," by David Finkelhor and Sharon Araji

About the Author:

Author and Speaker Sumi Mukherjee writes non-fiction books based on real life stories and speaks to audiences about the messages contained in his books. His focus is on bringing about positive changes in our society, with specific emphasis on prevention of bullying and child sexual abuse. Since October 2011, Sumi has been speaking to hundreds of people around the country so others can benefit from his stories. Sumi has spoken to teachers, counselors, administrators, social workers, school psychologists, mental health professionals, family members, caregivers, service providers, law enforcement professionals, students, parents, and the general audience. He has spoken at schools, colleges, religious organizations, bullying prevention conferences, other professional conferences (including School Social Workers Association conferences, School Psychologists Association Conference, Counseling Association Conferences, State Psychological Association Conferences), child abuse prevention conferences, domestic violence/sexual abuse/mental health awareness events. Sumi has spoken extensively all over the United States as well as in Canada.

Sumi was born in Calgary, Canada, and grew up in Minneapolis, Minnesota, USA. For more information please visit his website at www.authorsumi.com